ABOUT THE AUTHOR

Thomas Merton was born on 31 January 1915 in
Prades, southern France, to an American mother and
an artist father from New Zealand. The young Merton
was educated in the United States and France before
attending Oakham School in England. His mother
died when he was six and his father when he was
sixteen. After spending one year at Cambridge
University Merton moved to the United States to live
with his grandparents.

Merton entered the Catholic Church in 1938, during the period he was writing a master's thesis on
William Blake. Following some teaching at Columbia
University in New York City and at St. Bonaventure's
College, Olean, New York, Merton entered the
monastic community of the Abbey of Gethsemani at
Trappist, Kentucky, on 10 December 1941. He was
received by Abbot Frederic Dunne who encouraged
the young Frater Louis to translate works from the
Cistercian tradition and to write historical biographies
to make the Order better known. The abbot also urged
the young monk to write his autobiography, which was

published under the title *The Seven Storey Mountain* (1948). The book became an international bestseller, and was translated into twenty-eight languages. During the next twenty years, Merton wrote prolifically on a vast range of topics, including the contemplative life, prayer, and religious biographies. He became well known for his dialogue with other faiths and his stand on non-violence during the race riots and Vietnam War of the 1960s, and finally achieved the solitude he had long desired in a hermitage in 1965.

A new abbot allowed Merton the freedom to undertake a tour of Asia at the end of 1968, during which he met the Dalai Lama in India. He died by accidental electrocution in Bangkok, Thailand, while attending a meeting of religious leaders on 10 December 1968, just twenty-seven years to the day after his entrance into the Abbey of Gethsemani. His body was flown back to Gethsemani where he is buried. Since his death his influence has continued to grow and he is considered by many to be one of the greatest religious writers of the twentieth century.

Contemplative Prayer

THOMAS MERTON

Contemplative Prayer

DARTON · LONGMAN + TODD

Published in 2005 by
Darton, Longman and Todd Ltd
1 Spencer Court
140–142 Wandsworth High Street
London
SW18 4JJ

First published in Ireland under the title *The Climate of Monastic Prayer*,
no. 1 in the Cistercian Studies Series

First published in Great Britain in 1973 by Darton, Longman and Todd
This edition 2005

Ecclesiastical approval to publish this book was received from Ignace
Gillet, Abbot General of the Cistercian Order, and Bernard Flanagan,
Bishop of Worcester, 30 October 1968.

ISBN 0 232 52604 4

A catalogue record for this book is available from the British Library.

Printed and bound in Great Britain by
Page Bros, Norwich, Norfolk

LOUIS THOMAS MERTON
1915–1968

CONTENTS

FOREWORD
by A. M. Allchin

If Thomas Merton had not had an encounter with a faulty electric fan in Bangkok in December 1968, and if he had managed to avoid other such mishaps in the following years, he would have been 90 in 2005; not an impossible age for our long-lived generation, though old enough to make us feel a little of the distance between the 1960s and today.

This is a book which was written in the 1960s and first published in 1969 shortly after Merton's death. As with many of his writings, its textual history is more complicated than it seems. It is made up of at least two sections which had somewhat different origins. One section traces the development of the way of contemplative prayer, from the Desert Fathers through the Benedictine centuries of the monastic West down to the time of St. John of the Cross. In the other section we discover Merton wrestling to find the most adequate way to speak of the dread, the anxiety, the sense of darkness and emptiness which is often to be met at the heart of this way of prayer and which takes very particular forms in our own twentieth and twenty-first centuries.

This is the darkness in which we find that it is not we who know and love, but we who are known and loved. This is the hell in which we find in Isaac of Stella's remarkable words "a hell of mercy not of wrath". This darkness and dread may be full of perplexity but the way of prayer leads us to find beyond it an unexpected fullness.

> But true emptiness is that which transcends all things and yet is immanent in all. For what seems to be emptiness in this case is pure being. Or at least a philosopher might so describe it. But to the contemplative it is other than that. It is not this, not that. Whatever you say of it, it is other than what you say. The character of emptiness, at least for a Christian contemplative, is pure love, pure freedom. Love that is free of everything, not determined by any thing, or held bound by any special relationship. It is love for love's sake. It is sharing, through the Holy Spirit, in the infinite charity of God (pp. 118–19).

The book is thus, as often happens with Merton's writings, a text in which elements of the Christian tradition are brought to life for the present day, a text in which the present day is seen in a new perspective, because seen in the light of a long and living tradition.

What is true for the monk, Merton maintains, is true also in various ways for every Christian. Indeed he insists that his development of the theme in this book is essentially for our own time.

> After all, some of the basic themes of the existentialism of Heidegger, laying stress as they do on the ineluctable fact of death, on man's need for authenticity, and on a kind of spiritual liberation, can remind us that the climate in which monastic prayer flourished is not altogether absent from our modern world. Quite the contrary: this is an age that, by its very nature as a time of crisis, of revolution, of struggle, calls for the special searching and questioning which are the work of the monk in his meditation and prayer (pp. 24–5).

But perhaps we find these words themselves dated, coming to us from forty or more years ago, with their appeal to the work of a philosopher so much more renowned then than he is today? Do they truly belong to the twenty-first century? It will be for the reader to decide. To me at least it seems that the book does respond to our present situation, at times in an almost uncanny way. This is perhaps particularly the case in some of its most public and political allusions. It certainly seems to respond to our post-September 11th situation.

What could be more to the point at a time which is characterized on both sides of the Atlantic by a persistent religious rhetoric (more homely perhaps in its Texan phase, a little more sophisticated in the

Downing Street version) than Merton's insistence on the necessary *humility* of faith?

One thing is certain: the humility of faith, if it is followed by the proper consequences . . . will do far more to launch us into the full current of historical reality than the pompous rationalizations of politicians who think they are somehow the directors and manipulators of history. Politicians may indeed make history, but the meaning of what they are making turns out inexorably to have been something in a language they will never understand, which contradicts their own programs and turns all their achievements into an absurd parody of their promises and ideals (p. 140).

When we turn to the very next page of the book, to Merton's quotation from the commentary on the Lord's Prayer by Raïssa Maritain, almost the last of her writings, do we not find ourselves again confronting our own current situation?

If there were fewer wars, less thirst to dominate and to exploit others, less national egoism, less egoism of class and caste, if man were more concerned for his brother, and really wanted to collect together, for the good of the human race, all the resources which science places at his disposal especially today, there would be on earth fewer populations deprived of their necessary substance, there would be fewer children who die or are incurably weakened by undernourishment (p. 141).

When we turn back to the beginning of the book we can find in a new way Merton's original insistence on the prayer of the heart as being at the centre of all Christian monastic prayer and contemplation: "a way of keeping oneself in the presence of God and of reality, rooted in one's own inner truth." Here perhaps we find the secret of the threefold pattern of prayer which this book is setting out, a prayer which is truly *cosmotheandric*, and which interestingly corresponds to something deep in the heart of other religious traditions, a prayer keeping us rooted in the mystery of *God*, the reality of his *world*, which we meet all around us, and in the deepest *truth* of our own inmost being.

For the monk searches not only his own heart: he plunges deep into the heart of that world of which he remains a part although he seems to have "left" it. In reality the monk abandons the world only in order to listen more intently to the deepest and most neglected voices that proceed from its inner depth (p. 25).

"He who walks in darkness, to whom no light appears,
let him trust in the Name of Yahweh,
let him rely upon his God."

—Isaiah 50:10

"I will give them a heart to understand that I am Yahweh,
and they shall be my people and I will be their God
when they return to me with all their heart."

—Jeremiah 24:7

INTRODUCTION

The monk is a Christian who has responded to a special call from God, and has withdrawn from the more active concerns of a worldly life, in order to devote himself completely to repentance, "conversion," *metanoia*, renunciation and prayer. In positive terms, we must understand the monastic life above all as a life of prayer. The negative elements, solitude, fasting, obedience, penance, renunciation of property and of ambition, are all intended to clear the way so that prayer, meditation and contemplation may fill the space created by the abandonment of other concerns.

What is written about prayer in these pages is written primarily for monks. However, just as a book about psychoanalysis by an analyst and primarily for analysts may also (if it is not too technical) appeal to a layman interested in these matters, so a practical non-academic study of monastic prayer should be of interest to all Christians, since every Christian is bound to be in some sense a man of prayer. Though few have either the desire for solitude or the vocation to monastic life, all Christians ought, theoretically at least, to have enough interest in prayer to be able to read and make use of what is here said for monks, adapting it to the circumstances of their own vocation. Certainly, in the pressures of modern urban life, many will face the need for a certain interior silence and discipline simply to keep themselves together, to maintain their human and Christian identity and their spiritual freedom. To promote this they may often look for moments of retreat and prayer in which to deepen their meditative life. These pages discuss prayer in its very nature, rather than special restricted techniques. What is said here is therefore applicable to the prayer of any Christian, though perhaps with a little less emphasis on the intensity of certain trials which are proper to life in solitude.

Monastic prayer is, first of all, essentially simple. In primitive monasticism prayer was not necessarily liturgical, though liturgy soon came to be regarded as a specialty of monks and canons. Actually, the first monks in Egypt and Syria had only the most rudimentary liturgy, and their personal prayer was direct and uncomplicated. For example, we read in the sayings of the Desert Fathers[1] that a monk asked St. Macarius how to pray. The latter replied: "It is not necessary to use many words. Only stretch out your arms and say: Lord, have pity on me as you desire and as you well know how! And if the enemy presses you hard, say: Lord, come to my aid!" In John Cassian's *Conferences*

1. *Apothegmata*, 19, P.G. 34:249.

on Prayer[2] we see great stress laid by the early monks on simple prayer made up of short phrases drawn from the Psalms or other parts of Scripture. One of the most frequently used was *Deus in adjutorium meum intende,* "O God, come to my aid!"[3]

At first sight one might wonder what such simple prayers would have to do with a life of "contemplation." The Desert Fathers did not imagine themselves, in the first place, to be mystics, though in fact they often were. They were careful not to go looking for extraordinary experiences, and contented themselves with the struggle for "purity of heart" and for control of their thoughts, to keep their minds and hearts empty of care and concern, so that they might altogether forget themselves and apply themselves entirely to the love and service of God.

This love expressed itself first of all in love for God's Word. Prayer was drawn from the Scriptures, especially from the Psalms. The first monks looked upon the Psalter not only as a kind of compendium of all the other books of the Bible, but as a book of special efficacy for the ascetic life, in that it revealed the secret movements of the heart in its struggle against the forces of darkness.[4] The "battle Psalms" were all interpreted as referring to the inner war with passion and with the demons. Meditation was above all *meditatio scripturarum.*[5] But we must not imagine the early monks applying themselves to a very intellectual and analytical

2. *Conference* 10.
3. Psalm 69:2.
4. St. Athanasius, *Ep. ad Marcellinum.*
5. Cf. Dom Jean Leclercq, *Love of Learning and the Desire of God* (New York: Fordham University Press, 1961), Ch. I and IV.

"meditation" of the Bible. Meditation for them consisted in making the words of the Bible their own by memorizing them and repeating them, with deep and simple concentration, "from the heart." Therefore the "heart" comes to play a central role in this primitive form of monastic prayer.

St. Macarius was asked to explain a phrase of a Psalm: "The meditation of my heart is in your sight." He proceeded to give one of the earliest descriptions of that "prayer of the heart" which consisted in invoking the name of Christ, with profound attention, in the very ground of one's being, that is to say in "the heart" considered as the root and source of all one's own inner truth. To invoke the name of Christ "in one's heart" was equivalent to calling upon him with the deepest and most earnest intensity of faith, manifested by the concentration of one's entire being upon a prayer stripped of all non-essentials and reduced to nothing but the invocation of his name with a simple petition for help. Macarius said: "There is no other perfect meditation than the saving and blessed Name of Our Lord Jesus Christ dwelling without interruption in you, as it is written: 'I will cry out like the swallow and I will meditate like the turtledove!' This is what is done by the devout man who perseveres in invoking the saving Name of Our Lord Jesus Christ."[6]

The monks of the Oriental Churches in Greece and Russia have for centuries used a handbook of prayer called the *Philokalia*. This is an anthology of quotations from Eastern monastic Fathers from the third century

6. From Amelineau, quoted by Resch in *Doctrine Ascétique des Premiers Maitres Egyptiens*, p. 151.

to the Middle Ages, all concerned with this "prayer of the heart" or "prayer of Jesus." In the school of hesychastic contemplation which flourished in the monastic centers of Sinai and Mount Athos, this type of prayer was elaborated into a special, almost esoteric, technique. In the present study we will not go into the details of this technique which has at times (rather irresponsibly) been compared to yoga. We will only emphasize the essential simplicity of monastic prayer in the primitive "prayer of the heart" which consisted in interior recollection, the abandonment of distracting thoughts and the humble invocation of the Lord Jesus with words from the Bible in a spirit of intense faith. This simple practice is considered to be of crucial importance in the monastic prayer of the Eastern Church, since the sacramental power of the Name of Jesus is believed to bring the Holy Spirit into the heart of the praying monk. A typical traditional text says:

> A man is enriched by the faith, and if you will by the hope and humility, with which he calls on the most sweet Name of Our Lord Jesus Christ; and he is enriched also by peace and love. For these are truly a three-stemmed life-giving tree planted by God. A man touching it in due time and eating of it, as is fitting, shall gather unending and eternal life, instead of death, like Adam .... Our glorious teachers ... in whom liveth the Holy Spirit, wisely teach us all, especially those who have wished to embrace the field of divine silence (i.e. monks) and consecrate themselves to God, having renounced the world, to practice hesychasm with wisdom, and to prefer his mercy with undaunted hope. Such men would have,

as their constant practice, and occupation, the invoking of his holy and most sweet Name, bearing it always in the mind, in the heart and on the lips. . . .[7]

The practice of keeping the Name of Jesus ever present in the ground of one's being was, for the ancient monks, the secret of the "control of thoughts," and of victory over temptation. It accompanied all the other activities of the monastic life imbuing them with prayer. It was the essence of monastic meditation, a special form of that practice of the presence of God which St. Benedict in turn made the cornerstone of monastic life and monastic meditation. This basic and simple practice could of course be expanded to include the thought of the passion, death and resurrection of Christ, which St. Athanasius was among the first to associate with the different canonical hours of prayer.[8]

However, in the interests of simplicity, we will concentrate upon the most elementary form of monastic meditation, and will discuss prayer of the heart as a way of keeping oneself in the presence of God and of reality, rooted in one's own inner truth. We will appeal to ancient texts on occasion, but our development of the theme will be essentially modern.

After all, some of the basic themes of the existentialism of Heidegger, laying stress as they do on the ineluctable fact of death, on man's need for authenticity, and on a kind of spiritual liberation, can remind us that the climate in which monastic prayer flourished is not altogether absent from our modern world. Quite the

7. Kadloubovsky and Palmer, *Writings from the Philokalia on Prayer of the Heart*, pp. 172–173.
8. *De Virginitate*, 12-16.

contrary: this is an age that, by its very nature as a time of crisis, of revolution, of struggle, calls for the special searching and questioning which are the work of the monk in his meditation and prayer. For the monk searches not only his own heart: he plunges deep into the heart of that world of which he remains a part although he seems to have "left" it. In reality the monk abandons the world only in order to listen more intently to the deepest and most neglected voices that proceed from its inner depth.

This is why the term "contemplation" is both insufficient and ambiguous when it is applied to the highest forms of Christian prayer. Nothing is more foreign to authentic monastic and "contemplative" (e.g. Carmelite) tradition in the Church than a kind of gnosticism which would elevate the contemplative above the ordinary Christian by initiating him into a realm of esoteric knowledge and experience, delivering him from the ordinary struggles and sufferings of human existence, and elevating him to a privileged state among the spiritually pure, as if he were almost an angel, untouched by matter and passion, and no longer familiar with the economy of sacraments, charity and the Cross. The way of monastic prayer is not a subtle escape from the Christian economy of incarnation and redemption. It is a special way of following Christ, of sharing in his passion and resurrection and in his redemption of the world. For that very reason the dimensions of prayer in solitude are those of man's ordinary anguish, his self-searching, his moments of nausea at his own vanity, falsity and capacity for betrayal. Far from establishing one in unassailable narcissistic security, the way of prayer brings us face to face with the sham and indignity of the false self that seeks to live for itself alone and to enjoy the "consolation of prayer" for its own sake. This "self" is pure illusion, and ultimately he who lives for and by such an illusion must end either in disgust or in madness.

On the other hand, we must admit that social life, so-called "worldly life," in its own way promotes this illusory and narcissistic existence to the very limit. The curious state of alienation and confusion of man in modern society is perhaps more "bearable" because it is lived in common, with a multitude of distractions and escapes—and also with opportunities for fruitful action and genuine Christian self-forgetfulness. But underlying all life is the ground of doubt and self-questioning which sooner or later must bring us face to face with the ultimate meaning of our life. This self-questioning can never be without a certain existential "dread"—a sense of insecurity, of "lostness," of exile, of sin. A sense that one has somehow been untrue not so much to abstract moral or social norms but to one's own inmost truth. "Dread" in this sense is not simply a childish fear of retribution, or a naive guilt, a fear of violating taboos. It is the profound awareness that one is capable of ultimate bad faith with himself and with others: that one is living a lie.

The peculiar *monastic* dimension of this struggle lies in the fact that society itself, institutional life, organization, the "approved way," may in fact be encouraging us in falsity and illusion. The deep root of monastic "dread" is the inner conflict which makes us guess that in order to be true to God and to ourselves we must break with the familiar, established and secure norms and go off into the unknown. "Unless a man hate

26

father and mother. . . ." These words of Christ give some indication of the deep conflict which underlies all Christian conversion—the turning to a freedom based no longer on social approval and relative alienation, but on direct dependence on an invisible and inscrutable God, in pure faith.

It must be said at once that this struggle does not end at the gate of a monastery, and often it may come to light again in a conflict over one's monastic vocation. The purpose of monastic renewal and reform is to find ways in which monks and sisters can remain true to their vocation by deepening and developing it in new ways, not merely sacrificing their lives to bolster up antique structures, but channeling their efforts into the creation of new forms of monastic life, new areas of contemplative experience.

This is precisely the monk's chief service to the world: this silence, this listening, this questioning, this humble and courageous exposure to what the world ignores about itself—both good and evil. If, in the latter part of this study, we speak frequently of the concept of "dread," it will be in this existential sense.

The monk who is truly a man of prayer and who seriously faces the challenge of his vocation in all its depth is by that very fact exposed to existential dread. He experiences in himself the emptiness, the lack of authenticity, the quest for fidelity, the "lostness" of modern man, but he experiences all this in an altogether different and deeper way than does man in the modern world, to whom this disconcerting awareness of himself and of his world comes rather as an experience of boredom and of spiritual disorientation. The monk confronts his own humanity and that of his world at the deepest and most central point where the void seems to open out into black despair. The monk confronts this serious possibility, and rejects it, as Camusian man confronts "the absurd" and transcends it by his freedom. The option of absolute despair is turned into perfect hope by the pure and humble supplication of monastic prayer. The monk faces the worst, and discovers in it the hope of the best. From the darkness comes light. From death, life. From the abyss there comes, unaccountably, the mysterious gift of the Spirit sent by God to make all things new, to transform the created and redeemed world, and to re-establish all things in Christ.

This is the creative and healing work of the monk, accomplished in silence, in nakedness of spirit, in emptiness, in humility. It is a participation in the saving death and resurrection of Christ. Therefore every Christian may, if he so desires, enter into communion with this silence of the praying and meditating Church, which is the Church of the Desert.

I

THE climate in which monastic prayer flowers is that of the desert,[9] where the comfort of man is absent, where the secure routines of man's city offer no support, and where prayer must be sustained by God in the purity of faith. Even though he may live in a community, the monk is bound to explore the inner waste of his own being as a solitary. The Word of God which is his comfort is also his distress. The liturgy, which is his joy and which reveals to him the glory of God, cannot fill a heart that has not previously been humbled and emptied by dread. *Alleluia* is the song of the desert.

The Christian (even though he be a monk or a hermit) is never merely an isolated individual. He is a member of the praising community, the People of God. *Alleluia* is the victorious acclamation of the Risen Savior. Yet the People of God itself, while celebrating the praise of

9. Isaiah 35:1-10.

the Lord in a tabernacle of beauty overshadowed by the Bright Cloud of his presence, is still on pilgrimage. We acclaim God as members of a community that has been blessed and saved and is traveling to meet him as he comes in his promised Advent. Yet as individuals we know ourselves to be sinners. The prayer of the monk is dictated by this twofold consciousness of sin and redemption, wrath and mercy—as is the prayer of every Christian. But the monk is called to explore these two dimensions more thoroughly, and at greater cost, than his brothers who are devoted to works of mercy, or of creativity in the world.

In this study we are going to concern ourselves particularly with personal prayer, especially in its meditative and contemplative aspects. It is understood that the personal prayer of the monk is embedded in a life of psalmody, liturgical celebration and the meditative reading of Scripture (*lectio divina*). All this has both a personal and a communal dimension. We are concerned here most of all with the monk's own deepening existential grasp of his call to life in Christ, as it progressively reveals itself to him in the solitude where he is alone with God—whether or not his brothers may be physically present around him.

Dostoievski, in *The Brothers Karamazov*, shows us what Rozanov has called an "eternal conflict" in monasticism—and doubtless in Christianity itself. The conflict between the rigid, authoritarian, self-righteous, ascetic Therapont, who delivers himself from the world by sheer effort, and then feels qualified to call down curses upon it; and the Staretz, Zossima, the kind, compassionate man of prayer who identifies himself with the sinful and suffering world in order to call down God's blessing upon it.

It must be emphasized that in the present era of monastic renewal we are more and more concerned with the Zossima type. And this kind of monastic spirit is charismatic rather than institutional. It has much less need of rigid structures and is totally abandoned to one need alone: that of obedience to the word and spirit of God, tested by fruits of humility and compassionate love. Thus the Zossima type of monasticism can well flourish in offbeat situations, even in the midst of the world. Perhaps such "monks" may have no overt monastic connections whatever.

On the other hand, it must be admitted that communal structures have a value that must not be underestimated. The order, the quiet, the fraternal communication and love provided by a working and praying community are the obvious and ordinary place in which the life of prayer develops. Needless to say, such communities do not have to reproduce only the regular and observant patterns of Trappist, Carthusian or Carmelite convent life as we have known them hitherto.

II

IN THE way of prayer, as described by the early monastic writers, *meditatio* must be seen in its close relation to *psalmodia, lectio, oratio* and *contemplatio.* It is part of a continuous whole, the entire unified life of the monk, *conversatio monastica,* his turning from the world to God. To separate meditation from prayer, reading and contemplation is to falsify our picture of the monastic way of prayer. In proportion as meditation takes on a more contemplative character, we see that it is not only a *means* to an end, but also has something of the *nature* of an end. Hence monastic prayer, especially meditation and contemplative prayer, is not so much a way to find God as a way of resting in him whom we have *found,* who loves us, who is near to us, who comes to us to draw us to himself. *Dominus enim prope est.* Prayer, reading, meditation and contemplation fill the apparent "void" of monastic solitude and silence with the reality of God's presence, and thus we learn the true value of silence, and come to experience the emptiness and futility of those forms of distraction and useless communication which contribute nothing to the seriousness and simplicity of a life of prayer.

Whatever one may think of the value of communal celebration with all kinds of song and self-expression—and these certainly have their place—the kind of prayer we here speak of as properly "monastic" (though it may also fit into the life of any lay person who is attracted to it) is a prayer of silence, simplicity, contemplative and meditative unity, a deep personal integration in an attentive, watchful listening of "the heart." The response such prayer calls forth is not usually one of jubilation or audible witness: it is a wordless and total surrender of the heart in silence.

The inseparable unity of silence and monastic prayer was well described by a Syrian monk, Isaac of Niniveh:

Many are avidly seeking but they alone find who remain in continual silence. . . . Every man who delights in a multitude of words, even though he says admirable things, is empty within. If you love truth, be a lover of silence. Silence like the sunlight will illuminate you in God and will deliver you from the phantoms of ignorance. Silence will unite you to God himself. . . .

More than all things love silence: it brings you a fruit that tongue cannot describe. In the beginning we have to force ourselves to be silent. But then there is born something that draws us to silence. May God give you an experience of this "something" that is born of silence. If only you practice this, untold light will dawn on you in consequence . . . after a while a certain sweetness is born in the heart of this exercise and the body is drawn almost by force to remain in silence.

It must be observed that the term *mental* prayer is totally misleading in the monastic context. We rarely pray with the "mind" alone. Monastic meditation, prayer, *oratio*, contemplation and reading involve the whole man, and proceed from the "center" of man's being, his "heart" renewed in the Holy Spirit, totally submissive to the grace of Christ. Monastic prayer begins not so much with "considerations" as with a "return to the heart," finding one's deepest center, awakening the profound depths of our being in the presence of God who is the source of our being and our life.

In these pages, then, meditation will be used as more or less equivalent to what mystics of the Eastern Church have called "prayer of the heart"—at least in the general sense of a prayer that seeks its roots in the very ground of our being, not merely in our mind or our affections. By "prayer of the heart" we seek God himself present in the depths of our being and meet him there by invoking the name of Jesus in faith, wonder and love.

The term "mental prayer" unfortunately suggests a cleavage in the life of prayer between prayer "in the mind" with or without specific "acts" and simple vocal prayer, whether private or choral. This in turn implies another cleavage between public and private prayer. All sorts of problems are believed to flow from this supposed conflict. And, as a matter of fact, it is true that where one is convinced that there is a conflict between these "divisions" of the life of prayer, a kind of spiritual dislocation does result. But in early monastic tradition there was no such division, no such conflict. The whole life of the monk is a harmonious unity in which various forms of prayer have their proper time and place, but in which, in one way or another, the monk is considered as "praying always." St. Basil, for example, when he speaks of what modern writers call "private prayer" describes the prayer of the monk during his time of work. This prayer consists partly of Psalms, partly of the monk's own simple and spontaneous words—or wordless acts—directed to God.

> For prayer and psalmody every hour is suitable, that while one's hands are busy with their tasks we may praise God with the tongue, or, if not, with the heart. . . . Thus in the midst of our work we can fulfill the duty of prayer, giving thanks to him who has granted strength to our hands for performing our tasks, and cleverness to our minds for acquiring knowledge . . . thus we acquire a recollected spirit, when in every action we beg from God the success of our labors and satisfy our debt of gratitude to him . . . and when we keep before our minds the aim of pleasing him.[10]

In the Celtic tradition, a poem attributed to St. Columba describes the hermit life on an island in the ocean, and gives some idea of the various ways of prayer which unite the entire day's activities in an organic whole. After describing himself as an exile who

10. Long Rules, Q. 37, *Ascetical Works* (New York, 1950), p. 308.

has "turned his back on Eire" and who is moved to compunction by watching the waves break on the shore, he describes his delight in his life of sorrow and of praise:

That I might bless the Lord
Who conserves all—
Heaven with its countless bright orders,
Land, strand and flood,
That I might search the books all
That would be good for any soul;
At times kneeling to beloved Heaven
At times psalm-singing;
At times contemplating the King of Heaven,
Holy the Chief;
At times at work without compulsion,
This would be delightful;
At times picking kelp from the rocks
At times fishing
At times giving food to the poor
At times in a carcair (solitary cell).[11]

St. Bede also describes the constant meditation of the Celtic monks and laymen who accompanied St. Aidan in his mission to Northumbria in the seventh century. He ascribes the vital prayer-life of the monks to the fervor of Aidan himself:

His course of life was so different from the sloth-fulness of our times, that all those who accompanied him, whether they were tonsured monks or laymen,

11. Quoted by W. G. Hanson in Early Monastic Schools of Ireland (Cambridge, 1927), p. 22.

were employed in meditation, that is either in reading the Scriptures or pondering the Psalms. This was the daily employment of himself and all that were with him wheresoever they went.[12]

Note the broad meaning Bede gives to meditation, identifying it with *lectio* and psalmody. Note also that he sees no problem about monks and laymen living very much the same kind of simple prayer-life based on the Bible.

In these traditional texts we find not only a very simple, broad and sane view of the life of prayer, but one that is completely unified and yet diverse, in perfect harmony with nature. It is understood first of all that each one prays as he likes, whether vocally or "in his heart." Vocal prayer here means of course really singing the psalms out loud. This way of prayer is not a struggle to keep recollected *in spite of work,* travel or other activities, but flows from everyday life and is in accord with work and other duties: it is indeed an aspect of the monk's work, a climate in which the monk works, since it supposes a conscious awareness of and dependence on God. Once again, the forms taken by this "awareness" are not defined or prescribed. There is no hint that the monk must imagine God "out there" or *anywhere*; but each will proceed according to his own faith and his own capacity. The climate of this prayer is, then, one of awareness, gratitude and a totally obedient love which seeks nothing but to please God. We find the same simplicity in Chapter 52 of the *Rule* where St. Benedict talks of private and personal

12. *Historia Ecclesiastica*, III, 5.

prayer: "If anyone should wish to pray secretly, let him just go in and pray, not in a loud voice but with tears and fervor of heart." The climate of prayer suggested in this traditional expression, "tears and fervor of heart," is one of compunction and love.

The concept of "the heart" might well be analyzed here. It refers to the deepest psychological ground of one's personality, the inner sanctuary where self-awareness goes beyond analytical reflection and opens out into metaphysical and theological confrontation with the Abyss of the unknown yet present—one who is "more intimate to us than we are to ourselves."[13]

13. To adopt the phrase from Augustine's *Confessions.*

III

FROM these texts we see that in meditation we should not look for a "method" or "system," but cultivate an "attitude," an "outlook": faith, openness, attention, reverence, expectation, supplication, trust, joy. All these finally permeate our being with love in so far as our living faith tells us we are in the presence of God, that we live in Christ, that in the Spirit of God we "see" God our Father without "seeing." We know him in "unknowing." Faith is the bond that unites us to him in the Spirit who gives us light and love.

Some people may doubtless have a spontaneous gift for meditative prayer. This is unusual today. Most men have to learn how to meditate. There are *ways* of meditation. But we should not expect to find magical methods, systems which make all difficulties and obstacles dissolve into thin air. Meditation is sometimes quite difficult. If we bear with hardship in prayer and wait patiently for the time of grace, we may well discover that meditation and prayer are very joyful experiences. We should not, however, judge the value of our meditation by "how we feel." A hard and apparently fruitless meditation may in fact be much more valuable than one that is easy, happy, enlightened and apparently a big success.

There is a "movement" of meditation, expressing the basic "paschal" rhythm of the Christian life, the passage from death to life in Christ. Sometimes prayer, meditation and contemplation are "death"—a kind of descent into our own nothingness, a recognition of helplessness, frustration, infidelity, confusion, ignorance. Note how common this theme is in the Psalms.[14] If we need help in meditation we can turn to scriptural texts that express this profound distress of man in his nothingness and his total need of God. Then as we determine to face the hard realities of our inner life, as we recognize once again that we need to pray hard and humbly for faith, he draws us out of darkness into light—he hears us, answers our prayer, recognizes our need, and grants us the help we require—if only by giving us more faith to believe that he can and will help us in his own time. This is already a sufficient answer.

This alternation of darkness and light can constitute a kind of dialogue between the Christian and God, a dialectic that brings us deeper and deeper into the conviction that God is our all. By such alternations we grow in detachment and in hope. We should realize the great good that is to be gained only by this fidelity to meditation. A new realm opens up, that cannot be discovered otherwise: call it the "Kingdom of God." Any

14. See for instance Psalms 56, 39, etc.

effort and sacrifice should be made in order to enter this Kingdom. Such sacrifices are amply compensated for by the results, even when the results are not clear and evident to us. But effort is necessary, *enlightened,* *well-directed* and *sustained.*

Right away we confront one of the problems of the life of prayer: that of learning when one's efforts are enlightened and well-directed, and when they spring simply from our confused velleities and our immature desires. It would be a mistake to suppose that mere good will is, by itself, a sufficient guarantee that all our efforts will finally attain to a good result. Serious mistakes can be made, even with the greatest good will. Certain temptations and delusions are to be regarded as a normal part of the life of prayer, and when a person thinks he has attained to a certain facility in contemplation, he may find himself getting all kinds of strange ideas and he may, what is more, cling to them with a fierce dedication, convinced that they are supernatural graces and signs of God's blessing upon his efforts when, in fact, they simply show that he has gone off the right track and is perhaps in rather serious danger.

For this reason, humility and docile acceptance of sound advice are very necessary in the life of prayer. Though spiritual direction may not be necessary in the ordinary Christian life, and though a religious may be able to get along to some extent without it (many have to!), it becomes a moral necessity for anyone who is trying to deepen his life of prayer. Hence the traditional importance, in monastic life, of the "spiritual father," who may be the abbot or another experienced monk capable of guiding the beginner in the ways of prayer, and of immediately detecting any sign of misguided zeal and wrong-headed effort. Such a one should be listened to and obeyed, especially when he cautions against the use of certain methods and practices, which he sees to be out of place and harmful in a particular case, or when he declines to accept certain "experiences" as evidence of progress.

The right use of effort is determined by the indications of God's will and of his grace. When one is simply obeying God, a little effort goes a long way. When one is in fact resisting him (though claiming to have no other intention than that of fulfilling his will) no amount of effort can produce a good result. On the contrary, the stubborn ability to go on resisting God in spite of ever clearer indications of his will, is a sign that one is in great spiritual danger. Often the one who is concerned will not be able to see this himself. This is another reason why a spiritual father may be really necessary.

The work of the spiritual father consists not so much in teaching us a secret and infallible method for attaining to esoteric experiences, but in showing us how to recognize God's grace and his will, how to be humble and patient, how to develop insight into our own difficulties, and how to remove the main obstacles keeping us from becoming men of prayer.

Those obstacles may have very deep roots in our character, and in fact we may eventually learn that a whole lifetime will barely be sufficient for their removal. For example, many people who have a few natural gifts and a little ingenuity tend to imagine that they can quite easily learn, by their own cleverness, to master the methods—one might say the "tricks"—of the spiritual life. The only trouble is that in the spiritual life there are no tricks and no short cuts. Those who imagine that they can discover special gimmicks and put them to work for themselves usually ignore God's will and his grace. They are self-confident and even self-complacent. They make up their minds that they are going to attain to this or that, and try to write their own ticket in the life of contemplation. They may even appear to succeed to some extent. But certain systems of spirituality—notably Zen Buddhism—place great stress on a severe, no-nonsense style of direction that makes short work of this kind of confidence. One cannot begin to face the real difficulties of the life of prayer and meditation unless one is first perfectly content to be a beginner and really experience himself as one who knows little or nothing, and has a desperate need to learn the bare rudiments. Those who think they "know" from the beginning will never, in fact, come to know anything.

People who try to pray and meditate above their proper level, who are too eager to reach what they believe to be "a high degree of prayer," get away from the truth and from reality. In observing themselves and trying to convince themselves of their advance, they become imprisoned in themselves. Then when they realize that grace has left them they are caught in their own emptiness and futility and remain helpless. *Acedia* follows the enthusiasm of pride and spiritual vanity. A long course in humility and compunction is the remedy!

We do not want to be beginners. But let us be convinced of the fact that we will never be anything else but beginners, all our life!

IV

ANOTHER obstacle—and perhaps this one is more common—is spiritual inertia, inner confusion, coldness, lack of confidence. This may be the case of those who, after having made a satisfactory beginning, experience the inevitable let-down which comes when the life of meditation gets to be serious. What at first seemed easy and rewarding suddenly comes to be utterly impossible. The mind will not work. One cannot concentrate on anything. The imagination and the emotions wander away. Sometimes they run wild. At this point, perhaps, in the midst of a prayer that is dry, desolate and repugnant, unconscious fantasies may take over. These may be unpleasant and even frightening. More often, one's inner life simply becomes a desert which lacks all interest whatever.

This may no doubt be explained as a passing trial (the "night of the senses") but we must face the fact that it is often more serious than that. It may be the result of a wrong start, in which (due to the familiar jargon of books on prayer and the ascetic life) a cleavage has appeared, dividing the "inner life" from the rest of one's existence. In this case, the supposed "inner life" may actually be nothing but a brave and absurd attempt to evade reality altogether. Under the pretext that what is "within" is in fact real, spiritual, super-natural, etc., one cultivates neglect and contempt for the "external" as worldly, sensual, material and opposed to grace. This is bad theology and bad asceticism. In fact it is bad in every respect, because instead of accepting reality as it is, we reject it in order to explore some perfect realm of abstract ideals which in fact has no reality at all. Very often, the inertia and repugnance which characterize the so-called "spiritual life" of many Christians could perhaps be cured by a simple respect for the concrete realities of every-day life, for nature, for the body, for one's work, one's friends, one's surroundings, etc. A false supernaturalism which imagines that "the supernatural" is a kind of Platonic realm of abstract essences totally apart from and opposed to the concrete world of nature, offers no real support to a genuine life of meditation and prayer. Meditation has no point and no reality unless it is firmly rooted in *life*. Without such roots, it can produce nothing but the ashen fruits of disgust, *acedia,* and even morbid and degenerate introversion, masochism, dolorism, negation. Nietzsche pitilessly exposed the hopeless mess which results from this caricature of Christianity![15]

Beginners may get off to another kind of false start,

15. See Emmanuel Mounier, *The Spoils of the Violent.*

which ends up in a mixture of presumption and inertia. Having learned to enjoy some of the fruits of the spiritual life and having tasted some little success, when this is all lost to them they start looking around for reasons. They are convinced that someone is "to blame" and since they see no reason to blame themselves (for after all, perhaps it is not a matter of anyone being "to blame") they look for an explanation in the monastic society in which they live. Now we must admit that with monasticism in a full crisis of renewal, with all observances and even ideals called into question every day, there is no difficulty in finding things to criticize. The fact that the criticisms may have some basis does not, however, make them in every case entirely reasonable; especially when the criticism is purely negative and is resorted to principally as an outlet for frustration and resentment.

Many of the obstacles to the life of thought and love which is meditation come from the fact that people insist on walling themselves up inside themselves in order to cherish their own thoughts and their own experiences as a kind of private treasure. They misinterpret the gospel parable of the talents, and as a result they bury their talent in a napkin instead of putting it to work and increasing it. Even when we come to live a contemplative life, the love of others and openness to others remain, as in the active life, the condition for a living and fruitful inner life of thought and love. The love of others is a stimulus to interior life, not a danger to it, as some mistakenly believe.

Abbé Monchanin, a great contemplative of our time, a French priest who went to found a Christian ashram in southern India, said:

Let us keep alive the flame of thought and love: they are one and the same flame. Let us communicate to those around us the desire to understand and to give (and also to receive). There are too many walled-up consciences.[16]

Many serious and good monks, idealists, desire to make of their lives a work of art according to an approved pattern. This brings with it an instinct to study themselves, to shape their lives, to remodel themselves, to tune and re-tune all their inner dispositions—and this results in full-time meditation and contemplation of *themselves*. They may unfortunately find this so delightful and absorbing that they lose all interest in the invisible and unpredictable action of grace. In a word, they seek to build their own security, to avoid the *risk* and *dread* implied by submission to the unknown mystery of God's will.

Other obstacles:

Discouragement—we lose all confidence, become secretly convinced that we cannot get anywhere in prayer. In reality this too can be due to fatal subjectivism, which may have led us in the past to seek the wrong results—the cultivation of feelings and "fulfillment" on an immature level. There is danger of psychological regression here. If we are prepared to go forward, to *lose ourselves*, there is no need for discouragement. The remedy—*hope*.

Confusion, helplessness—a sense of incapacity again due to abuse of subjectivism—imprisoned in ourselves we become paralyzed. The way out is *faith*. What can

16. *Ecrits Spirituels*, p. 125.

we do about all these obstacles? The New Testament does not offer us techniques and expedients: it tells us to turn to God, to depend on his grace, to realize that the Spirit is given to us, wholly, in Christ. That he prays in us when we do not know how to pray:

If the Spirit of him who raised Jesus from the dead dwells in you, he who raised Christ Jesus from the dead will give life to your mortal bodies also through his Spirit which dwells in you. . . . For all who are led by the Spirit of God are sons of God. For you did not receive the spirit of slavery to fall back into fear, but you have received the spirit of sonship. When we cry "Abba! Father!" it is the Spirit himself bearing witness with our spirit that we are children of God. . . . Likewise the Spirit helps us in our weakness; for we do not know how to pray as we ought, but the Spirit himself intercedes for us with sighs too deep for words. And he who searches the hearts of men knows what is the mind of the Spirit, because the Spirit intercedes for the saints according to the will of God.[17]

The activity of the Spirit within us becomes more and more important as we progress in the life of interior prayer. It is true that our own efforts remain necessary, at least as long as they are not entirely superseded by the action of God "in us and without us" (according to a traditional expression). But more and more our efforts attain a new orientation: instead of being directed toward ends we have chosen ourselves,

17. Romans 8:11, 14-16, 26-27.

instead of being measured by the profit and pleasure we judge they will produce, they are more and more directed to an obedient and cooperative submission to grace, which implies first of all an increasingly attentive and receptive attitude toward the hidden action of the Holy Spirit. It is precisely the function of meditation, in the sense in which we speak of it here, to bring us to this attitude of awareness and receptivity. It also gives us strength and hope, along with a deep awareness of the value of interior silence in which the mystery of God's love is made clear to us.

V

THE Desert Father Ammonas, disciple of St. Anthony, said:

Behold, my beloved, I have shown you the power of silence, how thoroughly it heals and how fully pleasing it is to God. Wherefore I have written to you to show yourselves strong in this work you have undertaken, so that you may know that it is by silence that the saints grew, that it was because of silence that the power of God dwelt in them, because of silence that the mysteries of God were known to them.[18]

The prayer of the heart introduces us into deep interior silence so that we learn to experience its power. For that reason the prayer of the heart has to be always very simple, confined to the simplest of acts and often making use of no words and no thoughts at all.

18. Letter XII, P.O.XI, 606.

If on the other hand we speak of meditation as "mental prayer," consisting of busy discursive acts, complex logical reasoning, active imagining and the deliberate stirring up of affections, then we find, as St. John of the Cross shows, that this kind of meditation tends to conflict with our silent and receptive attention to the inner working of the Holy Spirit, especially if we attempt to carry on with it once its usefulness has come to an end. Misplaced effort in the spiritual life often consists in stubbornly insisting upon compulsive routines which seem to us to be necessary because they accord with our own short-sighted notions. St. John of the Cross maintains that this stubborn insistence cannot be cured by our own activity, and needs to be "purified" by God himself in the "night" of contemplation. He teaches that these misplaced efforts, and the faults of character and nature from which they spring, can only be removed by the secret purifying action of grace in the "dark night." Speaking of those who are guided, in their efforts, by the taste and esteem they have for their own individual and self-directed activity, St. John shows that it is precisely this attachment to their own ways of prayer and meditation that hinders their growth in the spiritual life:

The more spiritual a thing is the more wearisome they find it, for as they seek to go about spiritual matters with complete freedom and according to the inclination of their will, it causes them sorrow and repugnance to enter upon the narrow way, which, says Christ, is the way of life.[19]

19. *Dark Night*, I, vii, 4.

Here St. John supposes a complete contradiction between what is authentically spiritual (therefore simple and obscure) and what *appears* to these men to be spiritual because it excites and stimulates them psychologically.

God brings these people into the way of life by depriving them of the light and the consolation which they seek, by impeding their own efforts, by confusing and depriving them of the satisfactions which their own efforts aim to attain. Thus blocked and frustrated, unable to carry on with their accustomed projects, they find themselves in a very painful state in which their own wishes, their self-esteem, their presumption, their aggressivity and so on are systematically humiliated. What is worse, they cannot understand how this comes about! They do not know what is happening to them. It is here that they must decide whether to go on in the way of prayer under the secret guidance of grace, in the night of pure faith, or whether they will go back to a form of existence in which they can enjoy familiar routines and retain an illusory sense of their own perfect autonomy in perfectly familiar realms, without having to remain subject to the obedience of faith in these trying and baffling circumstances proper to the "dark night."

St. John of the Cross says that God brings these people into darkness—

> ... wherein he weans them from the breasts of these sweetnesses and pleasures, gives them pure aridities and inward darkness, takes from them all these superficialities and puerilities, and by very different means causes them to win the virtues. For however

assiduously the beginner practices the mortification in himself of all these actions and passions of his, he can never completely succeed—very far from it—until God works in him passively by means of the purgation of the said night.[20]

Here it might be well to recall briefly that for St. John of the Cross this "night" is by no means a pure negation. If it empties the mind and heart of the connatural satisfactions of knowledge and love on a simply human plane, it does so in order to fill them with a higher and purer light which is "darkness" to sense and to reason. The darkening is therefore at the same time an enlightenment. God darkens the mind only in order to give a more perfect light. The reason that the light of faith is darkness to the soul is, says St. John, that this is in reality an *excessive light*. Direct exposure to supernatural light darkens the mind and heart, and it is precisely in this way that, being led into the "dark night of faith," one passes from meditation, in the sense of active "mental prayer," to contemplation, or a deeper and simpler intuitive form of receptivity, in which, if one can be said to "meditate" at all, one does so only by receiving the light with passive and loving attention. So St. John of the Cross says:

For the soul, this excessive light of faith which is given it is thick darkness, for it overwhelms that which is great and it does away with that which is little, even as the light of the sun overwhelms all other lights whatsoever, so that when it shines and

20. *Dark Night*, I, vii, 5.

disables our power of vision they appear to be no lights at all. Even so the light of faith by its excessive greatness oppresses and disables that of the understanding; for the latter, of its own power, extends only to natural knowledge, although it has a faculty for the supernatural when Our Lord may be pleased to bring it to a supernatural action.[21]

The purpose of monastic prayer, psalmody, *oratio, meditatio,* in the sense of prayer of the heart, and even *lectio,* is to prepare the way so that God's action may develop this "faculty for the supernatural," this capacity for inner illumination by faith and by the light of wisdom, in the loving contemplation of God. Since the real purpose of meditation must be seen in this light, we can understand that a type of meditation which seeks only to develop one's reasoning, strengthen one's imagination and tone up the inner climate of devotional feeling has little real value in this context. It is true that one may profit by learning such methods of meditation, but one must also know when to leave them and go beyond to a simpler, more primitive, more "obscure" and more receptive form of prayer. If this "obscure" prayer becomes painfully dry and fruitless, one will do better to seek help from psalmody or from a few simple words of the Scriptures, than by resorting to the conventional machinery of discursive "mental prayer."

21. *Ascent of Mount Carmel,* II, iii, 1.

VI

THE early Christian tradition and the spiritual writers of the Middle Ages knew no conflict between "public" and "private" prayer, or between the liturgy and contemplation. This is a modern problem. Or perhaps it would be more accurate to say it is a pseudo-problem. Liturgy by its very nature tends to prolong itself in individual contemplative prayer, and mental prayer in its turn disposes us for and seeks fulfillment in liturgical worship.

Chapter 20 of the Rule of St. Benedict speaks of "Reverence in Prayer." It obviously concerns itself with the personal, individual prayer of the monk. It mentions a mental prayer (*oratio*) which is practiced by the community collectively, and this is to be made short. *Omnino brevietur*. Then the Rule asserts quite naturally that the individual monk may pray by himself. In Chapter 52 we read that "When the Work of God is finished let all go out in deep silence, and let reverence for God be observed, *so that any brother who wishes to pray privately may not be hindered by another's misbehavior*. And at other times also *if anyone wish to pray secretly, let him just go in and pray* not in a loud voice but with tears and fervor of heart." Returning to Chapter 20 we find this "secret" prayer characterized by several traditional expressions. It is "supplication" in "humility and with the devotion of purity." It is not characterized by much speaking (*non in multiloquio*) but by purity of heart, and tears of compunction. In a word, it ought to be "short and pure unless prolonged by the impulsion of divine grace."

This Chapter 20 of the Rule follows immediately on the Chapter about the Work of God, or liturgical prayer, in which the monk stands in the presence of God and of his angels and sings the psalms in such a way that his mind and voice may be in harmony.

These are all traditional expressions, and we know from the background of the Rule and from its main sources, for instance the *Institutes* and *Conferences* of John Cassian, that St. Benedict is simply expressing the classic monastic belief that secret and contemplative prayer should be inspired by liturgical prayer and should be the normal crown of that prayer. This is very important to remember, because for St. Benedict and the early monks the liturgy was not itself considered the "highest form of contemplation." On the contrary, Evagrius Ponticus, Cassian's master, held that psalmody was a work of the "active life" (*bios praktikos*) and that wordless contemplative prayer in purity of heart, without images or words, even beyond thoughts, could be expected to flower from the active prayer of the liturgy as its normal fulfillment.

According to John Cassian, liturgical prayer bursts forth in a wordless and ineffable elevation of the mind and heart which he calls "fiery prayer"—*oratio ignita.* Here the "mind is illumined by the infusion of heavenly light, not making use of any human forms of speech but with all the powers gathered together in unity it pours itself forth copiously and cries out to God in a manner beyond expression, saying so much in a brief moment that the mind cannot relate it afterwards with ease or even go over it again after returning to itself."[22] Yet it is interesting that this is the conclusion of Cassian's commentary on the *Pater Noster.* "Fiery prayer" is just the normal fruition that bursts forth, by the grace of God, when vocal prayer is well made. "The Lord's Prayer (says Cassian in the same chapter) leads all who practice it well to that higher state and brings them at last to the prayer of fire (*ignita oratio*) which is known and experienced by few and which is an inexpressibly high degree of prayer."

This may not be exactly what St. Benedict himself had in mind. We suspect that the Patriarch of Monte Cassino was thinking of a much simpler and less ecstatic kind of "purity."

Turning to Evagrius, we can quote a classical sentence on the prayer of the progressive who is "getting close to true theology." Here we know we are "close" "when the understanding, in ardent love for God, begins bit by bit to go forth from the flesh and casts aside all thoughts that come from the senses, the

22. *Conference* 9, Ch. 24.

memory or the temperament, while at the same time being filled with respect and joy."[23]

Cassian and Evagrius do not belong to the Benedictine tradition. They are, however, at its source, as is also St. Basil, who might be quoted here.

As a matter of fact, St. Basil is very businesslike in the treatment of prayer. He is more concerned with the organization of the prayer–life of the ascetic or the pattern of the canonical hours than he is with private prayer. It is to be noted in any case that Basil's so-called "Rules" are spiritual directories for ascetic communities of a purposely different character from the cenobitic and eremitical monasticism of Egypt. Basil is thinking more of a religious life that we today would call "active," and he is in consistent and explicit reaction against the purely contemplative, ascetic and solitary way of the Egyptian monks. The ascetics of Basil retain more contact, if not with the "world" then certainly at least with the Christian community which they serve to some extent in works of charity and mercy.

Basil is then not so much interested in promoting long hours of contemplation as in discouraging an appetite for contemplation which, if it interfered with work and the normal duties of life, he would regard as inordinate.

Private prayer for Basil is then prayer that is carried on *while the ascetic is at work* or going about his ordinary duties:

For prayer and psalmody every hour is suitable, that while one's hands are busy with their tasks we may

23. *De Oratione*, n. 61.

praise God sometimes with the tongue, or if not, with the heart. . . . Thus in the midst of our work we can fulfill the duty of prayer, giving thanks to him who has granted strength to our hands for performing our tasks, and cleverness to our minds for acquiring knowledge. . . . Thus we acquire a recollected spirit, when in every action we beg from God the success of our labors and satisfy our debt of gratitude to him . . . and when we keep before our minds the aim of pleasing him.[24]

After this he speaks of the communal prayer of the canonical hours. Here it can be seen that St. Basil's idea of prayer fits into the context of what is traditionally known as the active life. This is not the *theoria* or the *theologia* of Evagrius Ponticus, nor is it the *Hesychia* of the Byzantine contemplatives who, though doubtless spiritual sons of Basil, were rather in the tradition of Sinai than that of the Long Rules.

Obviously, Basil is talking of manual work, which can quite easily be united with any form of prayer. But how about more "distracting" occupations, such as the apostolic ministry?

24. Long Rules, Q. 37—*Ascetical Works* (New York, 1950), p. 308.

VII

ONE of the first Benedictines who began to look at
contemplative prayer as a problem, or as a factor
in monastic conflict, was St. Gregory the Great. In his
Dialogues, he had of course presented St. Benedict as
the charismatic model of perfect prayer, the father of
the monastic community who by his prayers and
prophetic insight guided the monks, protecting them
both spiritually and physically against the forces of
darkness. St. Benedict's death, standing in the monastic
church, sustained by the hands of his spiritual sons
while he receives the Body of Christ, is of course given
a very deep implicit significance by St. Gregory and by
Benedictine tradition after him. This death, which a
modern Benedictine authority believes to have taken
place on Holy Thursday, is at all events traditionally
regarded as the crowning event in a life dedicated to
liturgical worship.

However, we must not forget the even more significant incident of Benedict's vision, granted to him on the occasion of his customary solitary prayer in a tower room, where he meditated in the midnight hours, before the rest of the monks rose to chant the office. This too has a symbolic value, showing Benedict to be the type and model of solitary, monastic prayer. Anyone familiar with monastic tradition will immediately recognize that there is no such thing as a saintly pattern of the life of monastic prayer which does not necessarily contain this element of solitary contemplation, itself patterned on Christ's prayer alone on the mountain at night.

St. Gregory may have drawn the portrait of St. Benedict in broad idealistic strokes, creating so to speak an *ikon* of the charismatic father of monks and the man of prayer. But when he considered his own life, as he does very articulately in the *Moralia in Job*, he finds himself torn between the desire of his heart for solitary contemplation and his duty to devote his time and energy to active charity as "servant of the servants of God." As Dom Cuthbert Butler pointed out years ago, Gregory's treatment of the conflict between action and contemplation is "one of the most fundamental aspects of his theory of the monastic life. . . . As such it has profoundly influenced Benedictine life in subsequent ages. But no less profoundly has St. Gregory's teaching on the contemplative and active lives included all clerical life, of secular priests and religious alike, in the West."[25]

After describing the active life in terms one might expect, Gregory gives this classic definition of the contemplative life, which has so often been quoted in Benedictine literature that it has become almost a

25. *Western Mysticism*, 2nd edition, 1926, reprint 1951, p. 171.

commonplace of the Western monastic tradition. It should therefore be quoted again here:

> The contemplative life is to retain with all one's mind the love of God and neighbor *but to rest from exterior motion and cleave only to the desire of the Maker,* that the mind may now take no pleasure in doing anything, but having spurned all cares may be aglow to see the face of its Creator: so that it already knows how to bear with sorrow the burden. of the corruptible flesh, and with all its desires to seek to join the hymn-singing choirs of angels, to mingle with the heavenly citizens and to rejoice at its ever-lasting incorruption in the sight of God.[26]

Here we have a definition of contemplation that seems. to exclude activity, even of a spiritual nature. I say "seems to" exclude action. In fact contemplation should *transcend* action. However, this text, without any further explanation or qualification, stands as a contrast to the text quoted above from the Long Rules of St. Basil.

We are faced with a choice between two concepts which, though they might perhaps be reconcilable, are regarded as opposed. One an *active* idea of prayer: it accompanies work, and sanctifies work. The other a *contemplative* concept in which prayer, in order to penetrate more deeply into the mystery of God, must "rest from exterior action and cleave *only* to the desire of the Maker."

This distinction, whether we agree with it or not, exists in monastic tradition. But the tendency has been at times to forget the second concept altogether and to

26. Homilies of Ezechiel, II, ii, 7–8, trans. in Butler, *op. cit.*, p. 171.

present the Basilian idea of prayer-with-work as the genuine and the only really practicable way of personal contemplation. Well intentioned as this "solution" may have been, it ends in fact by reducing "contemplation" to another aspect of the active life and therefore in treating "activity-with-prayer" as synonymous with "contemplation."

Whatever we may think about this, it is not the idea of St. Gregory. For Gregory, the contemplative life is the heavenly life, which cannot be lived perfectly "in this world." But it is given to monks that they may begin in some measure to anticipate, by purity of heart, the "incorruption" of heaven. However, the active life which is germane to the present existence of man in the world always demands the attention even of those called to contemplation. In the first place, although (according to St. Gregory) the contemplative life is theoretically superior to and better than the active, and should be preferred to the active whenever possible, there are times when activity must supplant contemplation. Both are, in fact, demanded by charity, since man is commanded to love both God and his neighbor. Both necessarily must be combined in any earthly vocation, whether it be in the life of the pastor of souls or of the contemplative monk.

The only solution to the conflict between those two claims on our hearts is to achieve the balance that is required by our own individual vocation within the Church of God. The pastor of souls must not neglect the necessary element of prayer and meditation in his life. In theory the contemplative monk should prefer contemplation to action whenever he can legitimately do so, and when he leaves contemplation for action, it should only be because this is demanded by strict duty. In fact, it can be said that St. Gregory *encourages* the sense of anguish and conflict by saying that the contemplative should *regret* the necessity for action, even when it is posed as a matter of duty. Though a contemplative may be bound in charity to accept the office of bishop, he should never *seek* such an office, and should in fact dread it and try to avoid it in every legitimate and reasonable way. The principle applies to all "secular business" which is "to be borne with out of compassion but never sought for love."[27] So much for the theory of St. Gregory.

Let us frankly admit that this treatment of the question of action and contemplation seems to create greater and more serious problems than it solves. In point of fact Gregory was simply giving us the fruit of his own experience in a particular milieu, and not attempting to say the last word in this matter. Yet the Middle Ages took him with terrible seriousness. The vocation of the monk was to stay in his monastery and pray, and when he was called forth from the cloister, as he often was, to engage in church affairs, he was expected to go forth with weeping and lamentation, which he quite often sincerely did.

And so we find St. Bernard of Clairvaux, whose experience was quite similar to that of St. Gregory, taking up the same question in the twelfth century, and coming to rather similar conclusions. However, let us remember that while Pope St. Gregory wrote not only for monks but also for pastors (i.e. bishops), St. Bernard concerned himself almost entirely with monks.

27. *Regula Pastoralis,* ii, 7—Butler, *op. cit.,* p. 179.

VIII

IN THE monastic life one could find, according to
Bernard, three vocations: that of Lazarus the
penitent, that of Martha the active and devoted servant
of the monastic household, and that of Mary the contemplative. Mary had chosen (said St. Bernard) the
"best part," and there was no reason for her to envy
Martha or leave her contemplation, unasked, to share
in the labors of Martha. The portion of Mary is, by
nature, preferable to the other two and superior to them.
And one feels, reading between the lines of St. Bernard,
that this had to be said because it was not unknown for
Mary to envy Martha. The portion of Mary was not in
fact always desired by the majority.

St. Bernard himself solves the problem by saying that
after all Martha and Mary are sisters and they should
dwell together in the same household in peace. They
supplement one another. But in actual fact, true monastic perfection consists above all in the union of all three

vocations: that of the penitent, the active worker (in the care of souls above all) and the contemplative. But when Bernard speaks of the care of souls he refers to the duty of instructing and guiding other monks, rather than apostolic work outside the cloister. Yet the need for preachers and apostolic workers was acute in the twelfth century.

For St. Bernard, the contemplative life is that which is normal for the monk, it is that which he should always desire, always prefer, but the active life necessarily has its claims also. Contemplation should always be desired and preferred. Activity should be accepted, though never sought. In the end the perfection of the monastic life is found in the union of Martha, Mary and Lazarus in one person—usually such a person will be an abbot, like Bernard himself.[28]

It must not, of course, be imagined that either St. Gregory or St. Bernard is always concerned with contemplation from this problematical viewpoint. Because of the large amount of activity in their own lives they do, indeed, give ardent expression to their longing for the silence of contemplative prayer. Yet they always admit that contemplation is not unknown to them in their life of apostolic labor: indeed we sense that their contemplative experience is somehow deeper and richer precisely because of the mystical graces given to them to help them to preach to others.

But in any case, where contemplation forms part of a problem and a conflict, it is always in this real or imagined opposition to action which immediately arises

28. See Sermon 57, *Sermones in Cantica*, n. 10 –11, P.L. 183:1054–1055.

when contemplation is defined *a priori* as "rest from exterior action."

I know of no passage in which the modern "problem" of contemplation vs. liturgy is treated at length or taken seriously by the monastic Fathers. For them this problem did not exist. At worst, we might perhaps deduce it from the fact that Gregory and Bernard were never deprived of participation in liturgical offices of the Church except when they were on the road. Hence their laments about being deprived of "contemplation" are not laments over being deprived of "liturgy." And consequently by "contemplation" they seem to have meant something beyond liturgical prayer. However, I believe that to pursue this line of argument would lead only to confusion, in an issue where there is more than enough confusion already.

Let us simply consider what place St. Bernard allows to personal prayer *apart from the community*. Here the issue may seem picayune to the non-monastic reader. It was understood that the Cistercian monk could spend his time in contemplative prayer in the monastery church when the *Consuetudines* prescribed meditative reading or study in the cloister. That is not the question. The issue is whether or not a further element of solitude and (temporary) separation from the brethren was allowable. St. Bernard allows it, though with hesitation. The Cistercians were and are perhaps the order that has always insisted most strongly on the common, cenobitic life. But even in the Cistercian context St. Bernard can say:

Sit alone (*sede itaque solitarius*), have nothing in common with the crowd, nothing with the multitude of the others. . . . Holy soul, remain alone, and keep yourself for him alone out of all others.[29]

This use of the neo-platonic *topos*, "alone with the alone" is a little unusual in Bernard of Clairvaux. It is of course supported by the classical Gospel reference to Christ praying alone on the mountain. And in the mind of Bernard it refers first of all to interior solitude. Christ comes only in secret to those who have entered the inner chamber of the heart and closed the door behind them. And yet Bernard adds explicitly:

Nevertheless it will not be a waste of time to separate yourself even *physically* (*corpore*) when it can conveniently be done, especially at the time of prayer (*tempore orationis*).[30]

This refers not to any prescribed time for mental prayer, but to the moments when the monk will spontaneously want to pray by himself. It should be understood that according to monastic tradition the actions of the monk are not supposed to be entirely governed in their smallest detail by external regulations, but that there must also be left some room for the monk's own "rule of prayer" which will lead him, in response to the inspirations of grace, to give more time to prayer than the Rule actually prescribes, just as he will also do more than the Rule prescribes in matters like fasting and self-discipline. Here the monk is to be guided by interior inspirations of grace and by the exterior blessing of obedience. The two together can be taken as God's will

29. Sermon 40, *Sermones in Cantica*, n. 4, P.L. 183:983.
30. *Ibid.*

for him, in the planning of his own interior and contemplative life.

Peter the Venerable, St. Bernard's contemporary and Abbot of Cluny, was less hesitant and even more explicit than Bernard in encouraging solitary private prayer. Not only were monks of Cluniac houses granted permission to live in complete solitude as hermits or recluses, but *a fortiori* cenobites might be permitted to spend an exceptional amount of time praying or meditating in secluded places apart from the community. Peter the Venerable tells us in his *De Miraculis* (a kind of Cluniac *Fioretti*) of a certain Benedictine monk of his time who "used a little chapel in a remote and high part of a tower as though it were a cell, and who loved this more than any other part of the monastery for his place of prayer. There he remained day and night intent on divine contemplation (*divinae theoriae intentus*), with his mind he ascended above all mortal things, at all times in the company of the most blessed angels he stood, by interior vision, in the presence of the Creator."[31]

31. *De Miraculis* 1:20, P.L. 189:886.

IX

L ET us finally consult another Benedictine witness
of the twelfth century: Peter of Celles, one of the
most charming monastic writers of the Middle Ages.

Here again, as in the case of St. Gregory and St.
Bernard, we are face to face with a contemplative
personality, a talented, warm-hearted, intelligent man
who though he preferred the silence and meditation of
the cloister was called to be not only abbot but bishop.
It must be said at once that though Peter of Celles
experiences in himself the conflict between action and
contemplation, it does not concern or upset him. It is
less of a conflict. On the one hand, he can most earnestly
and seriously plead with Pope Alexander III for Henry,
Abbot of Clairvaux, who wants to refuse an episcopal
election. Peter tells the Pope quite frankly that it would
be a shame to deprive this monk of the "better part,"
the contemplative life, and throw him headlong into
the storms of the world. Episcopal business, for Peter,

is simply "the world." Peter seems quite frankly to praise and commend anyone who rejects the "burden" of activity and business in order to give himself to reading and meditation.

At the same time he sees that there are situations in which one must frankly face and accept the responsibilities and distractions of office and in such a case[32] he teaches a friend, recently appointed cardinal, how to deal with distracting thoughts.

It is particularly important to note that in Peter of Celles liturgical and personal contemplation exist side by side in perfect harmony. He can compose sermons in half hours snatched from the busy life of abbot, and they are brief meditations on the joy of the liturgical feasts. But he also enjoys the long nights of winter because they bring him added hours of leisure in which his mind is rested and refreshed in reading and silent contemplative prayer.[33]

He loves to describe the "sabbath" of contemplation, in which the soul rests in God and God works in the soul; the quiet and transcendent activity, the *quies sine rubigine,* in which purity of heart rewards the contemplative for the labor of asceticism. This labor is "active life" in another and older sense: the life of discipline, penance, mortification, which is absolutely necessary. Without virtue there can be no real and lasting contemplation. Without the labor of discipline there can be no rest in love.

But when asceticism has purified and liberated the inner man then, Peter says:

32. For instance, see *Epistola* 94, P.L. 202:542, 543.
33. *Epistola* 97, *ibid.*, col. 547.

God works in us while we rest in him. Beyond all grasping is this work of the Creator, itself creative, this rest. For such work exceeds all rest, in its tranquility. This rest, in its effect, shines forth as more productive than any work. Therefore let this action or rest of our contemplation be fashioned so as to reproduce, even though only in faint or sketchy lines, one model (of work and rest which is in God). . . . These things are not done in shadow or in night, but in the day, in the light, in the sun of justice; for he who snores in the night of vice cannot know the light of contemplation.[34]

In another place Peter of Celles compares active and contemplative prayer, showing them to be not so much in conflict as in harmony, completing one another. He uses the familiar figure of Jacob's two wives, Lia and Rachel, a trope which of course had been popularized long before by St. Gregory and all the Latin Fathers. The *oratio laboriosa* of active prayer cleanses us of sin, the *oratio devota* of contemplation is blessed by grace from heaven. Both, he says, are necessary. Neither one comes to the throne of grace without the other:

Prayer is laborious (active) when a man's heart is far away from him and God is far from the heart. Man's heart is far from him when it is occupied in superfluous cares or has grown cool in its religious fervor, or else when it is immersed in carnal desires. God too is far from the heart when he withdraws grace, withholds his presence, and tries the patience of the suppliant.

34. *Liber de Passibus*, P.L. 202:962.

Prayer is devout (contemplative) when grace comes quickly, when it fills the whole mind, when it is there before it is called for, when it gives us more than we can ask or understand.[35]

As St. John Chrysostom once said: "It is not enough to leave Egypt, one must also enter the Promised Land."[36] It might be mentioned that in this context "contemplative" prayer is taken in the broad sense and is not necessarily to be regarded as mystical.

35. *De Disciplina Claustrali*, 22, P.L. 202:1129.
36. *In Matthaei Evangelium* 39:4, P.G. 57:438.

X

LOOKING back over this brief survey of some characteristic writings in the "Benedictine centuries" we find, as we might expect, that prayer is the very heart of the monastic life. There is nowhere an explicit conflict between liturgical and private prayer; they both form part of a harmonious unity. There is, however, a conflict between the "active" and "contemplative" lives, though this conflict is more or less completely resolved by writers like Peter of Celles. They see, quite realistically and altogether in the spirit of St. Benedict himself, that all life on earth must necessarily combine elements of action and rest, bodily labor and mental illumination. It is sometimes necessary to practice a laborious, arid and unconsoling form of prayer; at others one may receive grace and light almost without effort, provided that he is sufficiently well disposed. This *vicissitude* (the term is from St. Bernard) or variation between labor and rest cuts across the dividing line between communal and private prayer, and is found, quite obviously, in both.

Hence, though liturgical prayer is by its nature more "active," it may at any moment be illuminated by contemplative grace. And though private prayer may tend by its nature to greater personal spontaneity, it may also be accidentally more arid and laborious than communal worship, which is in any case particularly blessed by the presence of Christ in the mystery of the worshipping community.

The doctrine of the early Benedictine centuries shows us then that the opposition between "official public prayer" and "spontaneous personal prayer" is largely a modern fiction. And this is true whether "official" prayer is regarded as the "true" and "contemplative" prayer, or whether these adjectives are chosen to dignify personal devotion.

How did the question arise? The answer to this difficult question may perhaps be guessed at in a brief consideration of the Benedictine prayer of the Counter-Reformation.

It would seem that the emphasis on "mental prayer" as a special, and especially *efficacious* exercise, became current and popular in the movement of monastic reform which began in the fifteenth century and became almost universal after the Council of Trent.

To take one example among many: Garcia de Cisneros (1455–1510), the Benedictine Abbot and reformer of Monserrat in Spain, is regarded as "the first Spanish mystic" (excluding the Catalan, Raymond Lull) and a precursor of St. Theresa and St. John of the Cross. He is also even more frequently regarded as a precursor of St. Ignatius Loyola and the "spiritual exercises."

Garcia de Cisneros was sent from Valladolid to undertake the reform of Monserrat by Ferdinand and Isabella. To aid and implement his reform he wrote two books, both of them manuals of prayer. Both are in the medieval Benedictine tradition.

One of these books was a *Directory of the Canonical Hours,* which attempted to reawaken the understanding of the divine office, and to enable the monks to chant it with fervor and understanding. The other aimed at reviving their spirit of personal and meditative prayer. It followed the traditional medieval pattern of the prayer-life divided between reading, meditation and contemplation, *lectio, meditatio, contemplatio.* It was also strongly influenced by the *devotio moderna* which left us so many devout treatises on the interior life, the most famous of which is the *Imitation of Christ.* This book on the interior life of the monk, by Garcia de Cisneros, was actually called the *Spiritual Exercises.* It was evidently much more popular and influential than his other work on the canonical hours.

Now it must be remembered that when a monastic reformer of the sixteenth century looked back to the immediate past for good and bad examples that might instruct him, he found the most vital and indisputable evidence of Christian prayer among the saints of the mendicant orders, including the tertiaries (like Catherine of Siena for instance) and also in the mystical movements which flourished more or less under the guidance of the mendicants: for example in Rhenish mysticism which centered in Dominican convents and was directed by Dominican theologians like Eckhart and Tauler.

When, as often happened, this mysticism was regarded with suspicion, the reformer could always fall back on the evidently "safe" *devotio moderna.*

When the monasteries of the Middle Ages lost their fervor the last observance that ceased to be properly carried out was the choral office. It may indeed have degenerated into a heartless routine, but the history of monasticism shows that long after the spirit of asceticism and of personal prayer has died in a monastery, the office may continue to be more or less devoutly and decently recited.

This has two important consequences for minds like those of the Counter-Reformation, faced with immediate and urgent problems. One is that reformers find themselves confronted with a more or less well organized structure of liturgy which, though the soul may have gone out of it, is still functioning in fairly good order. Hence it does not seem to require immediate attention. And so they look around for some other point at which to introduce the spearhead of reform. They conclude that where really strong and decisive action is needed is in the sphere of personal prayer and piety. Hence methods of meditation are taught, spiritual direction is given to guide the monk both in meditation and in self-discipline.

The patterns and ideals of the *devotio moderna,* with its insistence on personal devotion to the humanity of Christ, and on affective prayer, play an important role in these efforts. And hence there quite naturally arises the notion of a clear separation between personal fervor and liturgical prayer which is considered formal, official and public, and which can always be relied upon to provide a secure foundation of regularity in the life of prayer. But what is to be built on this foundation? Personal, affective piety. This means that even in the liturgical offices, the individual must begin to meditate on the passion of Christ (and this was not in itself alien to the oldest tradition). The conviction grows that a "fervent" monk in choir will do "more" than just "recite the office." He will add his own elements of affective prayer and even of contemplation. Hence it comes to be believed that the subjective element superadded to the liturgy is really more important and valuable than the objective liturgical worship itself.

In liturgical prayer, however, the objective element remains and is fundamental. So much so that it can even be regarded, in the "subjective" setting, as an "obstacle" to the "better" and more "fervent" personal prayer which the earnest reformer wants to superadd to it. Quite naturally one arrives at the conclusion that if one really wants to pray, one has to wait until the office is over, when spontaneous and subjective prayer can be given free rein.

Finally, when the laity also had become enthusiastic for meditation, affective prayer and devotions, and this requires priests who can direct them along the ways of the *devotio moderna,* then even priests in Benedictine monasteries are affected by the new trend and seek to become directors of mystical souls or at least teachers of meditation.

This brings us to the famous case of Dom Augustine Baker, one of the greatest of Benedictine "contemplatives" and a much-discussed figure. He is certainly the most revered and articulate master of the spiritual life produced by the English Benedictine Congregation until the present century when he has perhaps been equalled by Dom Chapman, who can be regarded as one of his disciples.

There are very many reasons why Dom Augustine Baker should have ended up as the truculent propounder of an absolute division between "active" and "contemplative" ways of prayer.

First of all, he was an English mystic in the tradition of the fourteenth century: that is to say he completed an already deeply ingrained English individualism with the permanent temperament of a confined recluse. Secondly, he had been exposed to "methods of meditation" in a reformed Italian Benedictine monastery. The methods nearly drove him out of his head. He found himself in a life-long conflict with those of his brethren for whom he coined the caustic and ambiguous expression: "the active livers." Finally, and perhaps this is the decisive factor, he became aware of the strong stand taken by St. Theresa and St. John of the Cross against the incalculable harm done to contemplatives by "active" directors who without any notion of the meaning of contemplation, imposed their systems on everyone tyrannically and without discernment.

Augustine Baker goes so far as to say that the real trouble with monasteries is that they are usually run by "active livers" who destroy the life of prayer by frustrating the lives of the contemplatives. This, we must submit, is perhaps a little extreme. Here is a characteristic passage:

There is no doubt that the decay of religion has principally proceeded from this preposterous disorder, viz. that in most religious communities active spirits have got the advantage to possess themselves of prelatures and spiritual pastorship over the con-templative, though the state of religion was instituted only for contemplation. And this has happened even since contemplative prayer has been restored by persons extraordinarily raised by God, as Ruys-broeck, Tauler, St. Theresa, etc. . . . Active spirits that live in religion, not being capable of such prayer as will raise them out of nature, have no apprehension of such employments (i.e. superiorship). On the contrary, being led by natural desires of pre-eminence and love of liberty, they do not fear to offer themselves, and even ambitiously to seek dominion over others, falsely in the meantime persuading themselves that their only motive is charity and the desire to promote the glory of God. . . . But what the effect is, experience shows.[37]

We can see here a subtle metamorphosis which, after the Counter-Reformation, has taken place in the context of the old traditional teaching on action and contempla-tion as it came from the pen of Gregory the Great. Doubtless the personal sensitivity and the harsh ex-periences of Dom Augustine contributed something to this new orientation. But in any case we have here reached a position which is not unfamiliar in modern times. Here action and contemplation are separated by a "great gulf" and there is no bridging the gap between them. For Dom Augustine, both liturgy and meditation were on the wrong side of the gulf. The real prayer was simple contemplative introversion, and this, to the average modern Benedictine who has espoused the

37. Baker, *Holy Wisdom* (London, n.d.), p. 177, slightly modernized.

cause of the liturgical movement, is just about as far as a monk can sink in degradation and betrayal. It bears the hideous stigma of quietism.

The unhappy result of this exaggerated division has been a great deal of confusion on both sides. But at the present time it is once again becoming clear that the problem is a false one and that the true vocation of the monks of the Benedictine family is not to fight for contemplation against action, but to restore the ancient, harmonious and organic balance between the two. Both are necessary. Martha and Mary are sisters. And, to repeat what we have quoted from Peter of Celles, neither can approach the throne of God without the other.

The answer is not liturgy alone, or meditation alone, but a full and many-sided life of prayer in which all these things can receive their proper emphasis. This emphasis will tend to differ in different persons, and in different individual vocations. It is the job of the father abbot to discern the various spirits and to encourage each in the way that is willed for him by the spirit of God. If necessary, obstacles must be removed and discreet adjustments can and should be made, so that the monastic community will produce a flowering of every spirit and every type of prayer.

What is said here for monks applies also, with certain adjustments, to all the faithful.

XI

WHAT is the purpose of meditation in the sense of "the prayer of the heart"?

In the "prayer of the heart" we seek first of all the deepest ground of our identity in God. We do not reason about dogmas of faith, or "the mysteries." We seek rather to gain a direct existential grasp, a personal experience of the deepest truths of life and faith, *finding ourselves in God's truth*. Inner certainty depends on *purification*. The dark night rectifies our deepest intentions. In the silence of this "night of faith" we return to simplicity and sincerity of heart. We learn *recollection* which consists in listening for God's will, in direct and simple attention to *reality*. Recollection is awareness of the unconditional. *Prayer* then means yearning for the simple presence of God, for a personal understanding of his word, for knowledge of his will and for capacity to hear and obey him. It is thus something much more than uttering petitions for good things external to our own deepest concerns.

Our desire and our prayer should be summed up in St. Augustine's words: *Noverim te, noverim me.*[38] We wish to gain a true evaluation of ourselves and of the world so as to understand the meaning of our life as children of God redeemed from sin and death. We wish to gain a true loving knowledge of God, our Father and Redeemer. We wish to lose ourselves in his love and rest in him. We wish to hear his word and respond to it with our whole being. We wish to know his merciful will and submit to it in its totality. These are the aims and goals of *meditatio* and *oratio*. This preparation for prayer can be prolonged by the slow, "sapiential" and loving recitation of a favorite psalm, dwelling on the deep sense of the words for us here and now.

In the language of the monastic fathers, all prayer, reading, meditation and all the activities of the monastic life are aimed at *purity of heart*, an unconditional and totally humble surrender to God, a total acceptance of ourselves and of our situation as willed by him. It means the renunciation of all deluded images of ourselves, all exaggerated estimates of our own capacities, in order to obey God's will as it comes to us in the difficult demands of life in its exacting truth. *Purity of heart* is then correlative to a new spiritual identity—the "self" as recognized in the context of realities willed by God—Purity of heart is the enlightened awareness of the new man, as opposed to the complex and perhaps rather disreputable fantasies of the "old man."

38. "May I know you, may I know myself!"

Meditation is then ordered to this new insight, this direct knowledge of the self in its higher aspect.

What am I? I am myself a word spoken by God. Can God speak a word that does not have any meaning?

Yet am I sure that the meaning of my life is the meaning God intends for it? Does God impose a meaning on my life from the *outside,* through event, custom, routine, law, system, impact with others in society? Or am I called to *create from within,* with him, with his grace, a meaning which reflects his truth and makes me his "word" spoken freely in my personal situation? My true identity lies hidden in God's call to my freedom and my response to him. This means I must use my freedom in order to *love,* with full responsibility and authenticity, not merely receiving a form imposed on me by external forces, or forming my own life according to an approved social pattern, but directing my love to the personal reality of my brother, and embracing God's will in its naked, often unpenetrable mystery.[39] I cannot discover my "meaning" if I try to evade the dread which comes from first experiencing my meaninglessness!

By meditation I penetrate the inmost ground of my life, seek the full understanding of God's will for me, of God's mercy to me, of my absolute dependence upon him. But this penetration must be authentic. It must be something genuinely *lived* by me. This in turn depends on the authenticity of my whole concept of my life, and of my purposes. But my life and aims tend to be artificial, inauthentic, as long as I am simply trying to adjust my actions to certain exterior norms of

39. Romans 11:33-36.

conduct that will enable me to play an approved part in the society in which I live. After all, this amounts to little more than learning a *role*. Sometimes methods and programs of meditation are aimed simply at this: learning to play a religious role. The idea of the "imitation" of Christ and of the saints can degenerate into mere *impersonation*, if it remains only exterior.

It is not enough for meditation to investigate the *cosmic order* and situate me in this order. Meditation is something more than gaining command of a *Weltan-schauung* (a philosophical view of the cosmos and of life). Even though such a meditation seems to bring about resignation to God's will as manifested in the cosmic order or in history, it is not deeply Christian. In fact, such a meditation may be out of contact with the deepest truths of Christianity. It consists in learning a few rational formulas, explanations, which enable one to remain resigned and indifferent in the great crises of life, and thus, unfortunately, it may make evasion possible where a direct confrontation of our nothingness is demanded. Instead of a stoical acceptance of "providential" decrees and events, and other manifestations of "law" in the cosmos, we should let ourselves be brought naked and defenceless into the center of that dread where we stand alone before God in our nothingness, without explanation, without theories, completely dependent upon his providential care, in dire need of the gift of his grace, his mercy and the light of faith.

We must approach our meditation realizing that "grace," "mercy" and "faith" are not permanent inalienable possessions which we gain by our efforts and retain as though by right, provided that we behave ourselves. They are *constantly renewed gifts*. The life of grace in our hearts is renewed from moment to moment, directly and personally by God in his love for us. Hence the "grace of meditation" (in the sense of "prayer of the heart") is also a special gift. It should never be taken for granted. Though we can say it is a "habit" which is in some sense permanently present to us, when we have received it, yet it is never something which we can claim as though by right and use in a completely autonomous and self-determining manner according to our own good pleasure, without regard for God's will—though we can make an autonomous use of our *natural* gifts. The gift of prayer is inseparable from another grace: that of humility, which makes us realize that the very depths of our being and life are meaningful and real only in so far as they are oriented toward God as their source and their end.

When we seem to possess and use our being and natural faculties in a completely autonomous manner, as if our individual ego were the pure source and end of our own acts, then we are in illusion and our acts, however spontaneous they may seem to be, lack spiritual meaning and authenticity.

Consequently: first of all our meditation should begin with the realization of our nothingness and helplessness in the presence of God. This need not be a mournful or discouraging experience. On the contrary, it can be deeply tranquil and joyful since it brings us in direct contact with the source of all joy and all life. But one reason why our meditation never gets started is perhaps that we never make this real, serious return to the center of our own nothingness before God. Hence we never enter into the deepest reality of our relationship with him.

In other words we meditate merely "in the mind," in the imagination, or at best in the desires, considering religious truths from a detached objective viewpoint. We do not begin by seeking to "find our heart," that is to sink into a deep awareness of the ground of our identity before God and in God. "Finding our heart" and recovering this awareness of our inmost identity implies the recognition that our external, everyday self is to a great extent a mask and a fabrication. It is not our true self. And indeed our true self is not easy to find. It is hidden in obscurity and "nothingness," at the center where we are in direct dependence on God. But since the reality of all Christian meditation depends on this recognition, our attempt to meditate without it is in fact self-contradictory. It is like trying to walk without feet.

Another consequence: even the capacity to recognize our condition before God is itself a grace. We cannot always attain it at will. To learn meditation does not, therefore, mean learning an artificial technique for infallibly producing "compunction" and the "sense of our nothingness" whenever we please. On the contrary, this would be the result of violence and would be inauthentic. Meditation implies the capacity to *receive* this grace whenever God wishes to grant it to us, and therefore a permanent disposition to humility, attention to reality, receptivity, pliability. To learn to meditate then means to gradually get free from habitual hardness of heart, torpor and grossness of mind, due to arrogance and non-acceptance of simple reality, or resistance to the concrete demands of God's will.

If in fact our hearts remain apparently indifferent and cold, and we find it morally impossible to "begin" meditating in this way, then we should at least realize that this coldness is itself a sign of our need and of our helplessness. We should take it accordingly as a motive for prayer. We might also reflect that perhaps without meaning to we have fallen into a spirit of routine, and are not able to see how to recover our spontaneity without God's grace, for which we must wait patiently, but with earnest desire. This waiting itself will be for us a school of humility.

XII

WITHOUT trying to make of the Christian life a cult of suffering for its own sake, we must frankly admit that self-denial and sacrifice are absolutely essential to the life of prayer.

If the life of prayer is to transform our spirit and make us "new men" in Christ, then prayer must be accompanied by "conversion," *metanoia*, that deep change of heart in which we die on a certain level of our being in order to find ourselves alive and free on another, more spiritual level.

St. Aelred of Rievaulx, writing to his sister, a recluse in Yorkshire, shows clearly the intimate relationship between meditation and asceticism:

The love of God requires two things: love in the heart (*affectus mentis*) and productive virtue (*effectus operis*). So we must work in the exercise of virtue and love in the sweetness of spiritual experience. The discipline of virtue consists in a certain way of life, in fasting, in vigils, in manual work, in reading, in prayer, in poverty and other such things. Our love is nourished on salutary meditation. And in order that this sweet love of Jesus may grow in your heart, you must practice a threefold meditation: in memory of the past, then awareness of present things, concern for future things.[40]

We must then control our thoughts and our desires. We must acquire interior freedom. This must of course not be misinterpreted. It does not mean that the Christian should regard the task of making a living in this world as a matter of no significance, still less that he can resign himself to a condition of social injustice and destitution, or encourage others to do so. Nor does it mean "contempt" for visible creation in a Manichean sense, as though sensible and material things were evil.

It means detachment and freedom with regard to inordinate cares, so that we are able to use the good things of life and able to do without them for the sake of higher ends. It means the ability to use or to sacrifice all created things in the interests of love. In St. Paul's words: "We have to be pure-minded, enlightened, forgiving and gracious to others; we have to rely on the Holy Spirit, on unaffected love, on the truth of our message, on the power of God. To the right and left we must be armed with innocence, now honored, now slighted, now traduced, now flattered. They call us deceivers and we tell the truth; unknown and we are freely acknowledged; dying men, and see we live; punished, yes, but not doomed to die; sad men that

40. *De Institutione Inclusarum,* n. 29.

rejoice continually; beggars that bring riches to many; disinherited, and the world is ours."[41]

This magnificent passage, sung by the Church in the Mass of the first Sunday of Lent, shows that the life of Christian asceticism leads us into a realm of paradox and apparent contradiction. The life of meditation is nourished by this paradoxical condition in which we are suspended between earth and heaven, due to our desire of renunciation, and due to the fact that this desire can never be fulfilled because it must remain within certain limits. Asceticism delivers us over to paradox, and meditation struggles with paradox. The issue of the struggle is the divine peace of spiritual love, in contemplation. But we cannot survive in this paradoxical state without special help from grace and without ever-renewed self-discipline.

Such exercises as fasting cannot have their proper effect unless our motives for practicing them spring from personal meditation. We have to think what we are doing, and the reasons for our action must spring from the depths of our freedom and be enlivened by the transforming power of Christian love. Otherwise, our self-imposed sacrifices are likely to be pretenses, symbolic gestures without real interior meaning. Sacrifices made in this formalistic spirit tend to be mere acts of external routine performed in order to exorcise interior anxiety and not for the sake of love. In that case, however, our attention will tend to fix itself upon the insignificant suffering which we have piously elected to undergo, and to exaggerate it in one way or the other, either to make it seem unbearable or else to

41. 2 Corinthians 6:6–10.

make it seem more heroic than it actually is. Sacrifices made in this fashion would be better left unmade. It would be more sincere as well as more religious to eat a full dinner in a spirit of gratitude than to make some picayune sacrifice of part of it, with the feeling that one is suffering martyrdom.

Our ability to sacrifice ourselves in a mature and generous spirit may well prove to be one of the tests of our interior prayer. Prayer and sacrifice work together. Where there is no sacrifice, there will eventually turn out to be no prayer, and vice versa. When sacrifice is an infantile self-dramatization, prayer will also be false and operatic self-display, or maudlin self-pitying introspection. Serious and humble prayer, united with mature love, will unconsciously and spontaneously manifest itself in a habitual spirit of sacrifice and concern for others that is unfailingly generous, though perhaps we may not be aware of the fact. Such a union of prayer and sacrifice is easier to evaluate in others than in ourselves, and when we become aware of this we no longer try to gauge our own progress in the matter.

XIII

TO understand what is now to follow, the reader will have to remember that the inner depths of the spiritual life are mysterious and inexplicable. They can hardly be described accurately in scientific language, and for that reason even theology barely touches on the subject, except in the poetic and symbolic language of the Fathers of the Church and of the Mystical Doctors.

John Tauler, for example, says that the unitive and mystical knowledge of God

is ineffable darkness and yet it is essential light. It is called an incomprehensible and solitary desert. This it certainly is; no one can find his way through it or see any landmarks for it has no marks which man can recognize. By "darkness" here you must understand a light which will never illuminate a created intelligence, a light which can never be naturally understood; and it is called "desolate" because there is no road which leads to it. To come there the soul must be led above itself, beyond all its comprehension and understanding. Then it can drink from the stream at its very sources, from those true and essential waters. Here the water is sweet and fresh and pure, as every stream is sweet at its source, before it has lost its cool freshness and purity.[42]

The unitive knowledge of God in love is not a knowledge of an object by a subject, but a far different and transcendent kind of knowledge in which the created "self" which we are seems to disappear in God and to know him alone. In passive purification then the self undergoes a kind of emptying and an apparent destruction, until, reduced to emptiness, it no longer knows itself apart from God.

Hence as we advance on the way of sacrifice we tend to submit more and more to a purifying action we cannot understand. The sacrifices that are not chosen are often of greater value than those we select for ourselves. Especially in meditation, we have to learn patience in the weary and arid path that takes us through dry places in prayer. Aridities grow more and more frequent, and more and more difficult as time goes on. In a certain sense, aridity can almost be taken as a sign of progress in prayer, provided it is accompanied by serious efforts and self-discipline. In the Prophecy of Hosea the Lord says that he will lead Israel into the wilderness and into the dry places in the valley of Achor, in order to speak to her heart and espouse her

42. Serm. XI for Monday in Passion Week, translated by Eric Coledge in *Spiritual Conferences of John Tauler* (St. Louis, 1961), p. 177.

to him in faith.[43] This promise follows upon the threat that Israel will be stripped of all her splendor and of the luxury which she has enjoyed in the surreptitious cult of false gods.

And she did not know that I have given her corn and wine and oil, and multiplied her silver, and gold, which they have used in the service of Baal. Therefore will I return, and take away my corn in its season, and my wine in its season, and I will set at liberty my wool, and my flax, which covered her disgrace. And now I will lay open her folly in the eyes of her lovers: and no man shall deliver her out of my hand: and I will cause her mirth to cease, her solemnities, her new moons, her sabbaths, and all her festival times. And I will destroy her vines, and her fig trees, of which she said: These are my rewards, which my lovers have given me: and I will make her as a forest, and the beasts of the field shall devour her. And I will visit upon her the days of Baalim, to whom she burnt incense, and decked herself out with earrings, and with her jewels, and went after her lovers, and forgot me, saith the Lord.[44]

In the tradition of Christian mysticism, a text like this can be applied to the purification of the mind and spirit of man in the aridity of prayer where spiritual consolations cease, thought becomes difficult and even impossible, and the imagination no longer obeys our will and our desires. At such a time, the interior senses and feelings dissociate themselves from our spiritual

43. Hosea 2:14, 15, 19.
44. Hosea 2:8–13.

effort and hinder us instead of helping us. The conscious mind begins to realize its lack of full autonomy and the unconscious makes its hidden power felt in obscure disturbances. All this is necessary to detach us from an immature way of prayer, and lead us to mature spiritual contemplation.

During the "dark night" of the feelings and senses, anxiety is felt in prayer, often acutely. This is necessary, because this spiritual night marks the transfer of the full, free control of our inner life into the hands of a superior power. And this too means that the time of darkness is, in reality, a time of hazard and of difficult options. We begin to go out of ourselves: that is to say, we are drawn out from behind our habitual and conscious defenses. These defenses are also limitations, which we must abandon if we are to grow. But at the same time they are, in their own way, a protection against unconscious forces that are too great for us to face naked and without protection.

If we set out into this darkness, we have to meet these inexorable forces. We will have to face fears and doubts. We will have to call into question the whole structure of our spiritual life. We will have to make a new evaluation of our motives for belief, for love, for self-commitment to the invisible God. And at this moment, precisely, all spiritual light is darkened, all values lose their shape and reality, and we remain, so to speak, suspended in the void.

The most crucial aspect of this experience is precisely the temptation to doubt God himself. We must not minimize the fact that this is a genuine risk. For here we are advancing beyond the stage where God made himself accessible to our mind in simple and primitive images. We are entering the night in which he is present without any image, invisible, inscrutable, and beyond any satisfactory mental representation.

At such a time as this, one who is not seriously grounded in genuine theological faith may lose everything he ever had. His prayer may become an obscure and hateful struggle to preserve the images and trappings which covered his own interior emptiness. Either he will have to face the truth of his emptiness or else he will beat a retreat into the realm of images and analogies which no longer serve for a mature spiritual life. He may not be able to face the terrible experience of being apparently without faith in order to really grow in faith. For it is this testing, this fire of purgation, that burns out the human and accidental elements of faith in order to liberate the deep spiritual power in the center of our being. This gift of God is, of itself, unattainable, but is given to us moment to moment, beyond our comprehension, by his inscrutable mercy.

Therefore, behold, I will allure her, and will lead her into the wilderness: and I will speak to her heart. . . . And it shall be that in that day, saith the Lord, that she shall call me "my husband," and she shall not call me "my Baal." And I will take away the names of Baalim out of her mouth, and she shall no more remember their name. . . . And I will espouse thee to me forever: and I will espouse thee to me in justice, and judgment, and in mercy, and in commiserations. And I will espouse thee to me in faith: and thou shalt know that I am the Lord.[45]

45. Hosea 2:14, 16, 17, 19, 20.

XIV

MEDITATION is not merely the intellectual effort to master certain *ideas about God* or even to impress upon our minds the mysteries of our Catholic faith. Conceptual knowledge of religious truth has a definite place in our life, and that place is an important one. Study plays an essential part in the life of prayer. The spiritual life needs strong intellectual foundations. The study of theology is a necessary accompaniment to a life of meditation. But meditation itself is not "study" and is not a purely intellectual activity. The purpose of meditation is not merely to acquire or to deepen objective and speculative knowledge of God and of the truth revealed by him.

In meditation we do not seek to know *about* God as though he were an object like other objects which submit to our scrutiny and can be expressed in clear scientific ideas. We seek to know God himself, beyond the level of all the objects which he has made and which confront us as "things" isolated from one another, "defined," "delimited," with clear boundaries. The infinite God has no boundaries and our minds cannot set limits to him or to his love. His presence is then "grasped" in the general awareness of loving faith, it is "realized" without being scientifically and precisely known, as we know a specimen under a microscope. His presence cannot be verified as we would verify a laboratory experiment. Yet it can be spiritually realized as long as we do not insist on verifying it. As soon as we try to verify the spiritual presence as an object of exact knowledge, God eludes us.

Returning to the classical passages of St. John of the Cross on the "dark night" of contemplation, we see that his doctrine about faith is often misrepresented. To some readers, he seems to be saying no more than that if you turn away from sensible and visible objects, you will come to see invisible objects. This is Neo-platonism, not the doctrine of St. John of the Cross. On the contrary, he teaches that the soul

> . . . must not only be in darkness with respect to that part that concerns the creatures and temporal things . . . *but likewise it must be blinded and darkened according to the part which has respect to God and spiritual things,* which is the rational and higher part. . . . It must be like to a blind man leaning upon dark faith, taking it for guide and light, and leaning upon none of the things that he understands, experiences, feels and imagines. For all these are darkness and will cause him to stray; and faith is above all that he understands, experiences, feels and imagines. And if he be not blinded as to this, and

remain not in total darkness, he attains not to that which is greater—namely, that which is taught by faith.[46]

Once again, however, this darkness is not merely negative. It brings with it an enlightenment which escapes the investigation and control of the understanding. "For who shall prevent God from doing that which he wills in the soul that is resigned, annihilated and detached?"[47]

This teaching of St. John of the Cross is not to be set aside merely as a peculiar form of "Carmelite spirituality." It is in the direct line of ancient monastic and patristic tradition, from Evagrius Ponticus, Cassian and Gregory of Nyssa on down through Gregory the Great and the followers of Pseudo-Dionysius in the West.

St. John Chrysostom writes of the "incomprehensibility of God":

Let us invoke him as the inexpressible God, incomprehensible, invisible and unknowable; let us avow that he surpasses all power of human speech, that he eludes the grasp of every mortal intelligence, that the angels cannot penetrate him nor the seraphim see him in full clarity, nor the cherubim fully understand him, for he is invisible to the principalities and powers, the virtues and all creatures without exception; *only the Son and the Holy Spirit know him.*[48]

St. Gregory of Nyssa describes the "mystical night":

46. *Ascent of Mount Carmel*, II, iv, 2.
47. *Ibid.*
48. *Incomprehensibility of God*, III, p. 166.

100

Night designates the contemplation (*theoria*) of invisible things after the manner of Moses who entered into the darkness where God was, this God who makes of darkness his hiding place.[49] Surrounded by the divine night the soul seeks him who is hidden in darkness. *She possesses indeed the love of him* whom she seeks, but the Beloved escapes the grasp of her thoughts. . . . *Therefore abandoning the search* she recognizes him whom she desires by the very fact that his knowledge is beyond understanding. Thus she says, "Having left behind all created things and abandoned the aid of the understanding, by faith alone I have found my Beloved. And I will not let him go, holding him with the grip of faith, until he enters into my bedchamber." The chamber is the *heart*, *which is capable* of the indwelling when it is restored to its primitive state.[50]

And Evagrius says (in the *Treatise on Prayer*, long attributed to St. Nilus): "Just as the light that shows us all has no need of another light in order to be seen, so God, who shows us all things, has no need of a light in which we may see him, for he is himself light by essence,"[51] and "See no diversity in yourself when you pray, and let your intelligence take on the impression of no form; but go immaterially to the immaterial and you will understand. . . . Aspiring to see the face of the Father who is in heaven, seek for nothing in the world to see a form or figure at the time of prayer."[52]

49. Psalm 17:12.
50. P.G. 44:892–893.
51. See Hausherr, *Les Leçons d'un Contemplatif* (Paris, 1960), p. 145.
52. *Ibid.*

Returning to the mystics of the Rhineland we find John Tauler saying typically: "All that a man rests in with joy, all that he retains as a good belonging to himself is all worm-eaten except for absolute and simple vanishing in the pure, unknowable, ineffable and mysterious good which is God, by renunciation of ourselves and of all that can appear in him."

And Ruysbroeck:

The interior man enters into himself in a simple manner, above all activity and all values, to apply himself to a simple gaze in fruitive love. There he encounters God without intermediary. And from the unity of God there shines into him a simple light. This simple light shows itself to be darkness, nakedness and nothingness. In this darkness, the man is enveloped and he plunges in a state without modes, in which he is lost. In nakedness, all consideration and distraction of things escape him, and he is informed and penetrated by a simple light. In nothingness he sees all his works come to nothing, for he is overwhelmed by the activity of God's immense love, and by the fruitive inclination of his Spirit he . . . becomes one spirit with God.[53]

The doctrine of purity of heart and "imageless" contemplation is summed up in the *Philokalia*: "That heart is pure which, always presenting to God a formless and imageless memory, is ready to receive nothing but impressions which come from him and by which he is wont to desire to become manifest to it."[54]

53. *The Adornment of the Spiritual Marriage*, II.
54. Kadloubovsky and Palmer, *Writings from the Philokalia* (London, 1957), p. 23.

In a word, God is invisibly present to the ground of our being: our belief and love attain to him, but he remains hidden from the arrogant gaze of our investigating mind which seeks to capture him and secure permanent possession of him in an act of knowledge that gives *power over him*. It is in fact absurd and impossible to try to grasp God as an object which can be seized and comprehended by our minds.

The knowledge of which we are capable is simply knowledge *about* him. It points to him in analogies which we must transcend in order to reach him. But we must transcend ourselves as well as our analogies, and in seeking to know him we must forget the familiar subject-object relationship which characterizes our ordinary acts of knowing. Instead we know him in so far as we become aware of ourselves as known through and through by him. We "possess" him in proportion as we realize ourselves to be possessed by him in the inmost depths of our being. Meditation or "prayer of the heart" is the active effort we make to keep our hearts open so that we may be enlightened by him and filled with this realization of our true relation to him. Therefore the classic form of "meditation" is repetitive invocation of the name of Jesus in the heart emptied of images and cares.

Hence the aim of meditation, in the context of Christian faith, is not to arrive at an objective and apparently "scientific" knowledge about God, but to come to know him through the realization that our very being is penetrated with his knowledge and love for us. Our knowledge of God is paradoxically a knowledge not of him as the object of our scrutiny, but of ourselves as utterly dependent on his saving and merciful knowledge of us. It is in proportion as we are known to him that we find our real being and identity in Christ. We know him in and through ourselves in so far as his truth is the source of our being and his merciful love is the very heart of our life and existence. We have no other reason for being, except to be loved by him as our Creator and Redeemer, and to love him in return. There is no true knowledge of God that does not imply a profound grasp and an intimate personal acceptance of this profound relationship.

The whole purpose of meditation is to deepen the consciousness of this basic relationship of the creature to the Creator, and of the sinner to his Redeemer.

It has been said above that the doctrine of mystical "unknowing," by which we ascend to the knowledge of God "as unseen" without "form or figure" beyond all images and indeed all concepts, must not be misunderstood as a mere turning away from the ideas of material things to ideas of the immaterial. The mystical knowledge of God, which already begins in a certain inchoative manner in living faith, is not a knowledge of immaterial and invisible essences as distinct from the visible and material. If in a certain sense *nothing* that we can see or understand can give us a fully adequate idea of God (except by remote analogy), then we can say that images and symbols and even the material which enters into sacramental signs and works of art regain a certain dignity in their own right, since they are no longer rejected in favor of other "immaterial" objects which are considered to be superior, as if they were capable of making us "see" God more perfectly. On the contrary, since we are well aware that images, symbols and works of art are only material, we tend to use them with greater freedom and less risk of error precisely because we realize the limitations of their nature. We know that they can only be means to an end, and we do not make "idols" out of them. On the contrary, today the more dangerous temptation is to raise ideas and ideologies to the status of "idols," worshipping them for their own sakes.

So we can say here, if only in passing, that image, symbol, art, rite and of course the sacraments above all, rightly and properly bring material things into the life of prayer and meditation, using them as means to enter more deeply into prayer. Denis de Rougement has called art "a calculated trap for meditation." The aesthetic aspect of the life of worship must not be neglected, especially today when we are barely recovering from an era of abomination and desolation in sacred art, due in part to a kind of manichaean attitude toward natural beauty on the one hand, and a rationalistic neglect of sensible things on the other. So, all that has been said above in quotations from St. John of the Cross and other doctors of Christian mysticism about "dark contemplation" and "the night of sense" must not be misinterpreted to mean that the normal culture of the senses, of artistic taste, of imagination, and of intelligence should be formally renounced by anyone interested in a life of meditation and prayer. On the contrary, such culture is *presupposed*. One cannot go beyond what one has not yet attained, and normally the realization that God is "beyond images, symbols and ideas" dawns only on one who has previously made a good use of all these things, who has a thorough and mature "monastic culture,"[55] and having reached the limit of symbol and idea goes on to a further stage in which he does without them, at least temporarily. For even if these human and symbolic helps to prayer lose their usefulness in the higher forms of contemplative union with God, they still have their place in the ordinary everyday life even of the contemplative. They form part of the environment and cultural atmosphere in which he usually lives.

The function of image, symbol, poetry, music, chant, and of ritual (remotely related to sacred dance) is to open up the inner self of the contemplative, to incorporate the senses and the body in the totality of the self-orientation to God that is necessary for worship and for meditation. Simply to neglect the senses and body altogether, and merely to let the imagination go its own way, while attempting to plunge into a deeply abstracted interior prayer, will end in no result even for one who is proficient in meditation.

All religious traditions have ways of integrating the senses, on their own level, into higher forms of prayer. The greatest mystical literature speaks not only of "darkness" and "unknowing" but also, and almost in the same breath, of an extraordinary flowering of "spiritual senses" and aesthetic awareness underlying and interpreting the higher and more direct union with

55. The term "monastic culture" is beginning to be seriously discussed today. It implies the development of a set of tastes and skills, of openness to certain specifically monastic values in all the arts and disciplines that have relation to the monastic life in all its fullness. One could say for example that for a twentieth-century Christian monk, "monastic culture" would imply not only an education in all that is living and relevant in monastic theology, tradition, and literature, as well as art, architecture, poetry, etc., but also in other religious cultures. Hence a certain knowledge of Zen, of Sufism, of Hinduism can rightly claim a place in the monastic culture of the modern monk of the West.

God "beyond experience." In fact, what is beyond experience has to be mediated, in some way, and interpreted in the ordinary language of human thought before it can be deeply reflected upon by the subject himself, and before it can be communicated to others. Of course, there is no denying that one may enter into deep contemplative prayer without being able to reflect on it, still less communicate anything whatever of the experience to others. But in mystical literature, which obviously implies communication through images, symbols and ideas, we find that contemplation in "unknowing" is generally accompanied by unusual poetic and theological gifts, whenever the fruit of contemplation is to be shared with others.

We find St. John of the Cross, for instance, describing the "Living Flame of Love" in very concrete and beautiful language which obviously reflects an even more concrete and beautiful experience which is here translated into symbolic terms. But he says without any ambiguity that what he is describing is "the savor of eternal life" and "an experience of the life of God" and the activity of the Holy Spirit. He says:

How can we we say that this flame wounds the soul, when there is nothing in the soul to be wounded, since it is wholly consumed by the fire of love? It is a marvelous thing: for, as love is never idle, but is continually in motion, it is continually throwing out sparks, like a flame, in every direction; and, as the office of love is to wound, that it may enkindle with love and cause delight, so, when it is as it were a living flame, within the soul, it is ever sending forth its arrow-wounds, like most tender sparks of delicate love, joyfully and happily exercising the arts and wiles of love. Even so, in his palace, at his marriage, did Ahasuerus show forth his graces to Esther his bride, revealing to her there his riches and the glory of his greatness. Thus that which the Wise Man said in Proverbs is now fulfilled in this soul, namely: I was delighted every day as I played before him always, playing over the whole earth, and my delight is to be with the sons of men, namely, by giving myself to them. Wherefore these wounds, which are the playing of God, are the sparks of these tender touches of flame which touch the soul intermittently and proceed from the fire of love, which is not idle, but whose flames, says the stanza, strike and wound

My soul in its deepest center.

For this feast of the Holy Spirit takes place in the substance of the soul, where neither the devil nor the world nor sense can enter; and therefore the more interior it is, the more it is secure, substantial and delectable; for the more interior it is the purer is it, and the more of purity there is in it, the more abundantly and frequently and widely does God communicate himself. And thus the delight and rejoicing of the soul and the spirit is the greater herein because it is God that works all this and the soul of its own power does naught therein; for the soul can do naught of itself, save through the bodily senses and by their help, from which in this case the soul is very free and very far removed; its only work is to receive God in the depths of the soul, who alone, without the aid of the senses, can move the soul in that which it does.[56]

When St. John of the Cross himself says that we must not attempt to attain to union with God by trying to conjure up images of such experiences in our hearts, he is obviously not invalidating what he has said in an attempt to communicate an experience of God *after* the fact. He is on the contrary trying to protect his reader against an egocentric and spiritually blind manipulation of images and concepts in order to attain to a supposed knowledge of God as an object which the mind of man can understand and enjoy on intellectual and aesthetic terms. There is indeed a certain kind of knowledge of God attained by images and reasoning but this is not at all the kind of experiential knowledge that St. John of the Cross describes. Indeed, the use of image and concept can become very dangerous in a climate of egocentricity and false mysticism.

The dangerous abuse of image and symbol is seen, for example, in the case of someone who tries to conjure up the "living flame" by an exercise of will, imagination and desire, and then persuades himself that he has "experienced God." In such a case, this obvious fabrication would be paid for dearly, because there is all the difference in the world between the *fruits* of genuine religious experience, a pure gift of God, and the results of mere imagination. As Jakob Boehme bluntly said: "Where does it stand in Scripture that a harlot can become a virgin by issuing a decree?"

The living experience of divine love and the Holy

56. *Living Flame of Love*, I, 8-9.

Spirit in the "flame" of which St. John of the Cross is speaking is a true awareness that one has died and risen in Christ. It is an experience of mystical renewal, an inner transformation brought about entirely by the power of God's merciful love, implying the "death" of the self-centered and self-sufficient ego and the appearance of a new and liberated self who lives and acts "in the Spirit." But if the old self, the calculating and autonomous ego, merely seeks to imitate the effects of such regeneration, for its own satisfaction and advantage, the effect is exactly the opposite—the ego seeks to confirm itself in its own selfish existence. The grain of wheat has not fallen into the ground and died. It remains hard, isolated and dry and there is no fruit at all, only a lying and blasphemous boast—a ridiculous pretense! If lying and fabrication are psychologically harmful even in ordinary relations with other men (a sphere where a certain amount of falsification is not uncommon) all falsity is disastrous in any relation with the ground of our own being and with God himself, who communicates with us through our own inner truth. To falsify our inner truth under pretext of entering into union with God would be a most tragic infidelity to ourselves first of all, to life, to reality itself, and of course to God. Such fabrications end in the dislocation of one's entire moral and intellectual existence.

XV

CONTEMPLATIVE prayer is, in a way, simply the preference for the desert, for emptiness, for poverty. One has begun to know the meaning of contemplation when he intuitively and spontaneously seeks the dark and unknown path of aridity in preference to every other way. The contemplative is one who would rather not know than know. Rather not enjoy than enjoy. Rather not have *proof* that God loves him. He accepts the love of God on faith, in defiance of all apparent evidence. This is the necessary condition, and a very paradoxical condition, for the mystical experience of the reality of God's presence and of his love for us. Only when we are able to "let go" of everything within us, all desire to see, to know, to taste and to experience the presence of God, do we truly become able to experience that presence with the overwhelming conviction and reality that revolutionize our entire inner life.

The fourteenth-century English mystic Walter Hilton says in his *Scale of Perfection*:

It is much better to be cut off from the view of the world in this dark night, however painful this may be, than to dwell outside occupied by the world's false pleasures. . . . For when you are in this darkness you are much closer to Jerusalem than when you are in the false light. Open your heart then to the movement of grace and accustom yourself to dwell in this darkness, strive to become familiar with it and you will quickly find peace, and the true light of spiritual understanding will flood your soul. . . .[57]

Contemplation is essentially a listening in silence, an expectancy. And yet in a certain sense, we must truly begin to hear God when we have ceased to listen. What is the explanation of this paradox? Perhaps only that there is a higher kind of listening, which is not an attentiveness to some special wave length, a receptivity to a certain kind of message, but a general emptiness that waits to realize the fullness of the message of God within its own apparent void. In other words, the true contemplative is not the one who prepares his mind for a particular message that he wants or expects to hear, but who remains empty because he knows that he can never expect or anticipate the word that will transform his darkness into light. He does not even anticipate a special kind of transformation. He does not demand light instead of darkness. He waits on the Word of God in silence, and when he is "answered," it is not so

57. *Scale of Perfection* (London, 1953), II, 25, p. 209.

much by a word that bursts into his silence. It is by his silence itself suddenly, inexplicably revealing itself to him as a word of great power, full of the voice of God.

But we must not take a purely quietistic view of contemplative prayer. It is not mere negation. Nor can a person become a contemplative merely by "blacking out" sensible realities and remaining alone with himself in darkness. First of all, one who does this of set purpose, as a conclusion to practical reasoning on the subject and without an interior vocation, simply enters into an artificial darkness of his own making. He is not alone with God, but alone with himself. He is not in the presence of the Transcendent One, but of an idol: his own complacent identity. He becomes immersed and lost in himself, in a state of inert, primitive and infantile narcissism. His life is "nothing," not in the dynamic, mysterious sense in which the "nothing," *nada*, of the mystic is paradoxically also the all, *todo*, of God. It is purely the nothingness of a finite being left to himself and absorbed in his own triviality.

The Rhenish mystics of the fourteenth century had to contend with many heretical forms of contemplation and both Tauler and Ruysbroeck carefully distinguished between the dark night of genuine contemplation and the arbitrary, self-willed passivity of those who adopt a quietistic form of prayer as a matter of systematic policy, simply cultivating inertia as though it were, by itself, sufficient to solve all problems. Of these, Tauler says:

These people have come to a dead end. They put their trust in this natural intelligence and they are thoroughly proud of themselves for doing so. They know nothing of the depths and riches of the life of Our Lord Jesus Christ. They have not even formed their own natures by the exercise of virtue and have not advanced along the ways of true love. They rely exclusively on the light of their reason and their bogus spiritual passivity.[58]

The trouble with quietism is that it cheats itself in its rationalization and manipulation of reality. It makes a cult out of "sitting still," as if this in itself had a magic power to solve all problems and bring man into contact with God. But in actual fact it is simply an evasion. It is a lack of honesty and seriousness, a trifling with grace and a flight from God. So much for "pure quietism." But does such a thing really exist in our day?

Absolute quietism is not exactly an ever-present danger in the world of our time. To be an out-and-out quietist, one would have to make heroic efforts to keep still and such efforts are beyond the power of most of us. However, there is a temptation to a kind of pseudo-quietism which afflicts those who have read books about mysticism without quite understanding them. And this leads them to a deliberately negative spiritual life which is nothing but a cessation of prayer, for no other reason than that one imagines that by ceasing to be active one automatically enters into contemplation. Actually, this leads one into a mere void without any interior, spiritual life, in which distractions and emotional drives gradually assert themselves at the expense of all mature, balanced activity of the mind and heart. To persist in this blank state could be very harmful spiritually, morally and mentally.

58. Sermon 52 in *Spiritual Conferences*, p. 233.

One who simply follows the ordinary ways of prayer, without any prejudice and without complications, will be able to dispose himself far better to receive his vocation to contemplative prayer in due time, assuming that he has one. True contemplation is not a psychological trick but a theological grace. It can come to us *only* as a gift, and not as a result of our own clever use of spiritual techniques.

The logic of quietism is a purely human logic in which two and two seem to make four. Unfortunately, the logic of contemplative prayer is of an entirely different order. It is beyond the realm of strict cause and effect because it belongs entirely to love, to freedom, and to spiritual espousal. In true contemplation, there is no "reason why" emptiness should necessarily bring us face to face with God. Emptiness might just as well bring us face to face with the devil, and as a matter of fact it sometimes does. This is part of the peril of this spiritual wilderness. The only guarantee against meeting the devil in the dark (if there can be said to be a guarantee at all) is simply our hope in God: our trust in his voice, our confidence in his mercy.

Hence the contemplative way is in no sense a deliberate "technique" of self-emptying in order to produce an esoteric experience. It is the paradoxical response to an almost incomprehensible call from God, drawing us into solitude, plunging us into darkness and silence, not to withdraw and protect us from peril, but to bring us safely through untold dangers by a miracle of love and power.

The contemplative way is, in fact, not a way. Christ alone is the way, and he is invisible. The "desert" of contemplation is simply a metaphor to explain the state of emptiness which we experience when we have left all ways, forgotten ourselves and taken the invisible Christ as our way. As St. John of the Cross says:

A soul is greatly impeded from reaching this high estate of union with God when it clings to any understanding or feeling or imagination or appearance or will or manner of its own, or to any other act of anything of its own, and cannot detach and strip itself of all these. . . . Wherefore upon this road, to enter upon the road is to leave the road; or to express it better, it is to pass on to the goal and to leave one's way and to enter upon that which has no way, which is God. For the soul that attains to this state has no longer any ways or methods, still less is it attached to such things or can it be attached to them . . . although it has within itself all ways, after the way of one who possesses nothing yet possesses all things.[59]

This might aptly be completed by the following words from John Tauler:

When we have tasted this in the very depth of our souls it makes us sink down and melt away in our nothingness and littleness. The brighter and purer the light shed on us by the greatness of God, the more clearly do we see our littleness and nothingness. In fact this is how we may discern the genuineness of this illumination; for it is the Divine God shining into our very being, not through images, not through our faculties, but in the very depths of our souls; its

59. *Ascent of Mount Carmel*, ii, 4.

effect will be to make us sink down more and more deeply into our own nothingness.[60]

There are two simple conclusions to be drawn from this. First, that contemplation is the summit of the Christian life of prayer, for the Lord desires nothing of us so much as to become, himself, our "way," our "truth and life." This is the whole purpose of his coming on earth to seek us, that he may take us, with himself, to the Father. Only in and with him can we reach the invisible Father, whom no man shall see and live. By dying to ourselves, and to all "ways," "logic" and "methods" of our own we can be numbered among those whom the mercy of the Father has called to himself in Christ. But the other conclusion is equally important. No logic of our own can accomplish this transformation of our interior life. We cannot argue that "emptiness" equals "the presence of God" and then sit down to acquire the presence of God by emptying our souls of every image. It is not a matter of logic or of cause and effect. It is not a matter of desire, of planned enterprise, or of our own spiritual technique.

The whole mystery of simple contemplative prayer is a mystery of divine love, of personal vocation and of free gift. This, and this alone, makes it true "emptiness" in which there is nothing left of ourselves.

An emptiness that is deliberately cultivated, for the sake of fulfilling a personal spiritual ambition, is not empty at all: it is full of itself. It is so full that the light of God cannot get into it anywhere; there is not a crack or a corner left where anything else can wedge itself into

60. *Loc. cit.*, p. 232.

117

this hard core of self-aspiration which is our option to live centered in our own self. Such "emptiness" is in fact the emptiness of hell. And consequently anyone who aspires to become a contemplative should think twice before he sets out on the road. Perhaps the best way to become a contemplative would be to desire with all one's heart to be anything but a contemplative; who knows?

But, of course, this is not true either. In the contemplative life, it is neither desire nor the refusal of desire that counts, but only that "desire" which is a form of "emptiness," that is to say which acquiesces in the unknown and peacefully advances where it does not see the way. All the paradoxes about the contemplative way are reduced to this one: being without desire means being led by a desire so great that it is incomprehensible. It is too huge to be completely felt. It is a blind desire, which seems like a desire for "nothing" only because nothing can content it. And because it is able to rest in no-thing, then it rests, relatively speaking, in emptiness. But not in emptiness as such, emptiness for its own sake. Actually there is no such entity as pure emptiness, and the merely negative emptiness of the false contemplative is a "thing," not a "nothing." The "thing" that it is is simply the darkness of self, from which all other beings are deliberately and of set-purpose excluded.

But true emptiness is that which transcends all things, and yet is immanent in all. For what seems to be emptiness in this case is pure being. Or at least a philosopher might so describe it. But to the contemplative it is other than that. It is not this, not that. Whatever you say of it, it is other than what you say. The character of emptiness, at least for a Christian contemplative, is pure love, pure freedom. Love that is free of everything, not determined by any thing, or held down by any special relationship. It is love for love's sake. It is a sharing, through the Holy Spirit, in the infinite charity of God. And so when Jesus told his disciples to love, he told them to love as universally as the Father who sends his rain alike on the just and the unjust. "Be ye perfect as your Heavenly Father is perfect." This purity, freedom and indeterminateness of love is the very essence of Christianity. It is to this above all that monastic prayer aspires.

XVI

WE are not only contingent beings, dependent on the love and will of a Creator whom we cannot know experientially except in so far as he reveals to us our personal relationship with him as his sons—we are also sinners who have *freely repudiated* this relationship. We have rebelled against him. The spirit of rebellious refusal persists in our heart even when we try to return to him. Much could be said, at this point, about all the subtlety and ingenuity of religious egoism which is one of the worst and most ineradicable forms of self-deception. Sometimes one feels that a well-intentioned and inculpable atheist is in many ways better off—and gives more glory to God—than some people whose bigoted complacency and inhumanity to others are signs of the most obvious selfishness! Hence we not only need to recover an awareness of our creaturehood; we also must repair the injury done to truth and to love by this repudiation, this infidelity. But how?

Humanly speaking, there is no way in which we can do this.

Our "nothingness" is then something more than the contingency of the creature. It is compounded with the *dread* of the sinner alienated from God and from himself, set in rebellious opposition to the truth of his own contingency and his own malice. More particularly, as a Palestinian monastic writer of the fifth century points out, the sense of loss, forsakenness and abandonment by God comes particularly to the man who is acting *contrary to the truth of his condition*:

> God does not abandon the negligent man who is negligent, nor the presumptuous man when he is presumptuous, but he abandons the devout man who becomes indifferent and the humble man when he is presumptuous. This is what is meant by sinning against one's condition. From this comes dereliction.[61]

The real import of dread is to be sought in an infidelity to a personal demand of which one is at least dimly aware: the failure to meet a challenge, to fulfill a certain possibility which demands to be met and fulfilled. The price of this failure to measure up to an existential demand of one's own life is a general sense of failure, of guilt. And it is important to remark that *this guilt is real*, it is not necessarily a mere neurotic anxiety. *It is the sense of defection and defeat that afflicts a man who is not facing his own inner truth and is not giving back to life, to God and to his fellow man, a fair return for all that has been given him.*

61. St. Dorotheus of Gaza.

However, the matter is immensely complicated by factors we cannot completely control or understand. Dread remains a mysterious and pervasive factor in all genuine spiritual growth, and one cannot "get rid" of it by any amount of impetuous action, no matter how generous. Dread is compounded with a certain helplessness and a dependence on grace, as well as with the after-effects of many other sins and errors. The experience of "dread," "nothingness" and "night" in the heart of man is then the awareness of infidelity to the truth of our life. More, it is an awareness of infidelity as unrepented and without grace as *unrepentable*. It is the deep, confused, metaphysical awareness of a *basic antagonism between the self and God* due to estrangement from him by perverse attachment to a "self" which is mysterious and illusory. Nor is this estrangement purely and simply a matter to be adjusted juridically *ex opere operato* by the reception of the sacraments with minimal good dispositions. True, he who receives the sacraments of the Church with proper dispositions can sincerely believe himself restored to the divine favor. But this will not liberate him from "dread" and "night" as long as he tends to cling to the empty illusion of a separate self, inclined to resist God. Nor will it effectively allay the sense of emptiness and nothingness which he will feel when left to himself without distraction (in the Pascalian sense) and without escape into routine or self-complacent rationalization.

Even the best of men, and perhaps especially they, when they return to a frank and undisguised self-awareness, confront themselves as naked, insufficient, disgruntled and malicious beings. They see their stubborn attachment to the lie in themselves, their disposition to infidelity, their fear of truth and of the risks it demands. This is all the more true when sincerity and a good life have removed those actual habits of sin which can be identified and rejected as sources of guilt and remorse. Even without acts of sin, we have in ourselves an *inclination* to sin and rebellion, an inclination to falsity and to evasion.

It is in some ways a comfort to be able to assign one's discontent to definite causes. *Remorse* is easier to bear than *dread*, for it is at least centered on something definite. But the worst emptiness is the emptiness of the faithful Christian who, when he has done what he had to do and has seriously sought God, responding conscientiously to the graces and tasks of life, still realizes even more acutely than before that he is an unprofitable servant. More than the sinner, more than the insincere one who can escape into the delusion of his own rightness, this man faces radical dread in his own being: the naked dread that is indefinite because it seems to be coextensive with his whole being and his whole life. Such a one sees that no virtue of his own, no good intentions, no ideals, no philosophy, no mystical elevation can rescue him from the futility, the apparent despair of his emptiness without God.

At the same time, he seems to lose the conviction that God is or can be a refuge for him. It is as if God himself were hostile and implacable or, worse still, as if God himself had become emptiness, and as if all were emptiness, nothingness, dread and night.

In the first place, because the light and wisdom of this contemplation are most bright and pure, and the soul which it assails is dark and impure, it follows that the soul suffers great pain when it receives it in itself, just as, when the eyes are dimmed by humours, and become impure and weak, they suffer pain through the assault of the bright light. And when the soul is indeed assailed by this Divine light, its pain, which results from its impurity, is immense; because, when this pure light assails the soul, in order to expel its impurity, the soul feels itself to be so impure and miserable that it believes God to be against it, and thinks that it has set itself up against God. This causes it so much grief and pain (because it now believes that God has cast it away) that one of the greatest trials which Job felt when God sent him this experience, was as follows, when he said: Why have you set me against you, so that I am grievous and burdensome to myself? For, by means of this pure light, the soul now sees its impurity clearly (although darkly), and knows clearly that it is unworthy of God or of any creature. And what gives it most pain is that it thinks that it will never be worthy and that its good things are all over for it. This is caused by the profound immersion of its spirit in the knowledge and realization of its evils and miseries; for this divine and dark light now reveals them all to the eye, that it may see clearly how in its own strength it can never have aught else. In this sense we may understand that passage from David, which says: For iniquity you have corrected man and have undone his soul: he is consumed as by the spider.[62]

It is natural for one in this case to dread the loss of his faith, indeed of his own integrity and religious

62. *Dark Night of the Soul*, II, V, 5.

identity, and to cling desperately to whatever will seem to preserve the last shreds of belief. So he struggles, sometimes frantically, to recover a sense of comfort and conviction in formulated truths or familiar religious practices. His meditation becomes the scene of this *agonia*, this wrestling with nothingness and doubt. But the more he struggles the less comfort and assurance he has, and the more powerless he sees himself to be. Finally he loses even the power to struggle. He feels himself ready to sink and drown in doubt and despair.

This is not the moment for arrogance or proud thrusts of will. The arrogant man will break in the agony of darkness. His meditation will be intolerable, and he will either revolt or despair. We must also recognize that one of the causes of mental or emotional breakdown of novices and young monks is that they tend to get too quickly into this state of confusion and dereliction, perhaps by unwisely and presumptuously pushing themselves too far, but more often because of a lack of identity and spiritual maturity. The man of today is more and more vulnerable in this respect. His efforts to seek peace and light are carried on not in a realm of relative security, in a geography of certitude, but over the face of a thinly-veiled abyss of disoriented nothingness, into which he quickly falls when he finds himself without the total support of reassuring and familiar ideas of himself and of his world. Nevertheless, it is precisely this support that we must learn to sacrifice.

This is the genuine climate of serious meditation, in which, without light and apparently without strength, even seemingly without hope, we commit ourselves to an entire surrender to God. We drop our arrogance, we submit to the incomprehensible reality of our situation and we are content with it because, senseless though it may seem, it makes more sense than anything else. We begin to realize, at least obscurely, the truth of what the Desert Father, St. Ammonas, said: "If God did not love you he would not bring temptations upon you. . . . For the faithful, temptation is necessary, for all those who are free of temptation are not among the elect."[63] Here then we make not the confident and conspicuously generous resolutions of our moments of light, but we abandon ourselves in submission, colorlessness, hiddenness, humility and distress to the will of God. We see there is no hope but in him, and we leave *everything* finally in his hands. "Take heed," said Jakob Boehme, "of putting on Christ's purple mantle without a resigned will."

This deep dread and night must then be seen for what it is: not as punishment, but as purification and as grace. Indeed it is a great gift of God, for it is the precise point of our encounter with his fullness.

Dread is an expression of our insecurity in this earthly life, a realization that we are never and can never be completely "sure" in the sense of *possessing* a definitive and established spiritual status. It means that we cannot any longer hope in ourselves, in our wisdom, our virtues, our fidelity. We see too clearly that all that is "ours" is nothing, and can completely fail us. In other words we no longer rely on what we "have," what has been given by our past, what has been required. We are open to God and to his mercy in the inscrutable future and our trust is entirely in his grace,

63. *Letters*, ed. Kmosko, P.O. XI., p. 591.

which will support our liberty in the emptiness where we will confront unforeseen decisions. Only when we have descended in dread to the center of our own nothingness, by his grace and his guidance, can we be led by him, in his own time, to find him in losing ourselves.

The fourth-century monk Ammonas describes the testing of the man of prayer by dereliction and dread, following the "fruitful" and consoling experiences of the beginners. It is this dread that proves the real seriousness of our love of God and prayer, for those who simply fall into coldness and indifference show they have little real desire to know him. Ammonas says:

God flies from them and abandons them to see whether they seek him or not. There are some who, when the Spirit has fled from them, and abandoned them, remain heavy and without movement in this torpor. They do not pray God to lift this weight off them and to send them the joy and sweetness they knew before, but because of their negligences they become strangers to the sweetness of God. Thus they are carnal and are content to wear the monastic habit while denying its power by their lives. They are the ones who have been blinded in their life and who do not understand the work of God. . . . If God sees that they implore him with sincerity and with their whole heart, and if he sees that they really deny their own will he gives them a greater joy than they had before and strengthens them even more.[64]

The dread and dereliction of the spiritual man is then a kind of hell but it is, in the words of Isaac of Stella (a

64. Quoted in *Dictionnaire de Spiritualité*, vol. IV, col. 348.

twelfth-century Cistercian), a "hell of mercy and not of wrath": *In inferno sumus, sed misericordiae, non irae; in caelo erimus.*[65] To be in a "hell of mercy" is to fully experience one's nothingness, but in a spirit of repentance and surrender to God with desire to accept and do his will, not in a spirit of diffuse hatred, disgust and rebellion even though these may be *felt* at times on the superficial level of emotion. It is in this "hell of mercy" that in finally relaxing our determined grasp of our empty self, we find ourselves lost and liberated in the infinite fullness of God's love. We escape from the cage of emptiness, despair, dread and sin into the infinite space and freedom of grace and mercy. But if there remains any vestige of self that can be aware of itself as "having arrived" and having "attained possession," then it can be sure of the return of the old dread, the old night, the old nothingness, until all self-sufficiency and self-complacency are destroyed.

> The haughty looks of man shall be brought low, and the pride of men shall be humbled; and the Lord alone will be exalted in that day. For the Lord of hosts has a day against all that is proud and lofty, against all that is lifted up and high. And the haughtiness of man shall be humbled, and the pride of men shall be brought low; and the Lord alone will be exalted in that day. And the idols shall utterly pass away.[66]

> We destroy arguments and every proud obstacle to the knowledge of God, and take every thought captive to obey Christ.[67]

65. Sermon 27, P.L. 194:1780.
66. Isaiah 2:11, 12, 17, 18.
67. 2 Corinthians 10:5.

XVII

FROM this we can see what makes a good meditation and what makes a bad one. All methods of meditation that are, in effect, merely devices for allaying and assuaging the experience of emptiness and dread are ultimately evasions which can do nothing to help us. Indeed, they may confirm us in delusions and harden us against that fundamental awareness of our real condition, against the truth for which our hearts cry out in desperation.

What we need is not a false peace which enables us to evade the implacable light of judgment, but the grace courageously to accept the bitter truth that is revealed to us; to abandon our inertia, our egoism and submit entirely to the demands of the Spirit, praying earnestly for help, and giving ourselves generously to *every effort asked of us by God*.

A method of meditation or a form of contemplation that merely produces the illusion of having "arrived somewhere," of having achieved security and preserved one's familiar status by playing a part, will eventually have to be unlearned in dread—or else we will be confirmed in the arrogance, the impenetrable self-assurance of the Pharisee. We will become impervious to the deepest truths. We will be closed to all who do not participate in our illusion. We will live "good lives" that are basically inauthentic, "good" only as long as they permit us to remain established in our respectable and impermeable identities. The "goodness" of such lives depends on the security afforded by relative wealth, recreation, spiritual comfort, and a solid reputation for piety. Such "goodness" is preserved by routine and the habitual avoidance of serious risk—indeed of serious challenge. In order to avoid apparent evil, this pseudo-goodness will ignore the summons of genuine good. It will prefer routine duty to courage and creativity. In the end it will be content with established procedures and safe formulas, while turning a blind eye to the greatest enormities of injustice and uncharity.

Such are the routines of piety that sacrifice everything else in order to preserve the comforts of the past, however inadequate and however shameful they may be in the present. Meditation, in such a case, becomes a factory for alibis and instead of struggling with the sense of falsity and inauthenticity in oneself, it battles against the exigencies of the present, armed with platitudes minted in the previous century. If necessary, it also fabricates condemnations and denunciations of those who risk new ideas and new solutions.

XVIII

SO FAR we have concentrated on the personal experience of emptiness that accompanies the deepening
of serious faith. The question may now be raised: is
this really relevant to the true spirit of monastic
prayer? Is all this talk of dread, the desert, nothingness,
poverty, simply an excuse for the negativism and
inertia of a subjective spirit? Is this not after all only an
alibi for spiritual sterility? Would it not be more honest
to forget about this futile emphasis on personal and
meditative prayer and concentrate on the objective
worship of the Church's liturgy in which there is
supposedly no problem?

The argument continues: objective participation in
the mysteries of Christ as celebrated by the Christian
community takes the person out of himself, raises him
above the level of self-preoccupation in which he is
plagued by "dread." Why dignify a common and
neurotic anxiety with an existential label, and thus

perpetuate in our monasteries the delusion of narcissistic piety?

The answer to this would be that the emptiness and
inner poverty we have been discussing are not just
symptoms of modern neurosis and self-concern. Nor are
they confined merely to personal and interior prayer.
They manifest themselves also in our experience of
liturgy. They have been commonly treated, in
monastic tradition, as the "fear of the Lord" which is
the beginning of wisdom, and they are inseparable
from that basic humility which St. Benedict places at
the very foundation not only of the monk's whole life[68]
but also of all his prayer, whether liturgical[69] or
meditative.[70] The dread of falsity and inauthenticity can
indeed create extremely complex problems in liturgy
and community life where there may be a problem not
only of individuals but of the community itself. After
all, some of the most agonizing questions of our time
are those which probe into the heart of the monastic
communities, parishes, Catholic Action groups and
indeed the Church herself. It is no simple matter to
face the "dread" that arises out of a serious confrontation with infidelity on a community level—infidelity in
which all are implicated and which no individual can
honestly negotiate merely by denouncing others or by
walking out on them.

It must be said that without a profoundly serious and
urgent sense of our condition as sinners and of our
helplessness without God's grace, liturgical prayer
itself would be a trifling exercise in aestheticism and

68. Rule, Ch. 7.
69. *Ibid.*, Ch. 19.
70. *Ibid.*, Ch. 20.

self-distraction. Indeed, the biblical texts used through-
out the liturgy, particularly those from the Psalms
and the Prophets, portray in the strongest terms man's
dread and anguish in separation from God, and man's
desperate need of grace and salvation. New Testament
texts in their turn speak of the salvation and light that
have come to man through the Cross of Christ. The
whole liturgy is animated by the movement of descent
and ascent which is that of the Christian Pasch, the
Easter Mystery of our death and resurrection with
Christ.

Unless the Christian participates to some degree in
the dread, the sense of loss, the anguish, the dereliction
and the destitution of the Crucified, he cannot really
enter into the mystery of the liturgy. He can neither
understand the rites and prayers, nor appreciate the
sacramental signs and enter deeply into the grace they
mediate. Father Monchanin has wisely observed the
emptiness of a certain superficial optimism which freely
distributes clichés about the "sense of history" and
evades the reality of dread by plunging into ceaseless
and generally useless activity. They prove themselves
to be blind agents, he says, by the very emptiness of
their efforts. "For us," Fr. Monchanin continues, "let
it be enough to know ourselves to be in the place God
wants for us (in the modern world) and carry on our
work, even though it be no more than the work of an
ant, infinitesimally small, and with unforseeable results.
Now is the hour of the garden and the night, the hour
of silent offering: *therefore the hour of hope:* God
alone. Faceless, unknown, unfelt, yet undeniable:
God."[71]

71. *Ecrits Spirituels,* 126.

Let us frankly recognize the true import and the true challenge of the Christian message. The whole gospel kerygma becomes impertinent and laughable if there is an easy answer to everything in a few external gestures and pious intentions. Christianity is a religion for men who are aware that there is a deep wound, a fissure of sin that strikes down to the very heart of man's being. They have tasted the sickness that is present in the inmost heart of man estranged from his God by guilt, suspicion and covert hatred. If that sickness is an illusion, then there is no need for the Cross, the sacraments and the Church. If the Marxists are right in diagnosing this human dread as the expression of guilt and inner dishonesty of an alienated class, then there is no need to preach Christ any more, and there is no need either of liturgy or of meditation. History has yet to show the Marxists are right in this matter however, since by advancing on their own crudely optimistic assumptions they have unleashed a greater evil and a more deadly falsity in man's murderous heart than anyone except the Nazis. And the Nazis, in their turn, borrowed from Nietzsche a similar false diagnosis of the Christian's "fear of the Lord." It is nevertheless true that the spirit of individualism, associated with the culture and economy of the West in the Modern Age, has had a disastrous effect on the validity of Christian prayer. But what is meant by individualism in the life of prayer?

The interior life of the individualist is precisely the kind of life that closes in on itself without dread, and rests in itself with more or less permanent satisfaction. It is to some extent immune to dread, and is able to take the inevitable constrictions and lesions of an inner life complacently enough, spiriting them away with devotional formulas. Individualism in prayer is content precisely with the petty consolations of devotionalism and sentimentality. But more than that, individualism resists the summons to communal witness and collective human response to God. It shuts itself up and hardens itself against everything that would draw it out of itself. It refuses to participate in what is not immediately pleasing to its limited devotional tastes here and now. It remains centered and fixed upon a particular form of consolation which is either totally intimate or at best semi-private, and prefers this to everything else precisely because it need not and cannot be shared.

The purpose of this fixation (which can be maintained with a stubborn will and a minimum of faith) is to produce reassurance, a sense of spiritual identity, an imaginary fulfillment, and perhaps even an excuse for evading the realities of life.

It is unfortunately all too true that bogus interiority has saved face for pious men and women who were thus preserved from admitting their total non-entity. They have imagined that they were capable of love just because they were capable of devout sentiment. One aspect of this convenient spiritual disease is its total insistence on ideals and intentions, in complete divorce from reality, from act, and from social commitment. Whatever one interiorly desires, whatever one dreams, whatever one imagines: that is the beautiful, the godly and the true. Pretty thoughts are enough. They substitute for everything else, including charity, including life itself.

It is precisely the function of dread to break down this glass house of false interiority and to deliver man from it. It is dread, and dread alone, that drives a man out of this private sanctuary in which his solitude becomes horrible to himself without God. But without dread, without the disquieting capacity to see and to repudiate the idolatry of devout ideas and imaginings, man would remain content with himself and with his "inner life" in meditation, in liturgy or in both. Without dread, the Christian cannot be delivered from the smug self-assurance of the devout ones who know all the answers in advance, who possess all the clichés of the inner life and can defend themselves with infallible ritual forms against every risk and every demand of dialogue with human need and human desperation.

This individualist piety is then a poor substitute for true personalism. It robs man of the power to put himself free, without care, at the disposal of other persons (the *disponibilité* of Gabriel Marcel). But only this freedom of self-disposal in openness, without after-thought, can enable man to find himself as a person. It is precisely this freedom, this openness, which is essential for fully mature participation in liturgical worship. This power of self-surrender is not gained except through the experience of that dread which afflicts us when we taste the awful dereliction of the soul closed in upon itself.

It would consequently be a serious error to ignore the true meaning of inner meditative prayer and its crucial importance for the whole Christian life, especially for the full understanding of liturgy. In any case, we are not speaking here of the prayer of the heart as an isolated, particular exercise, as a separate department of the devout life. The prayer of the heart must penetrate every aspect and every activity of Christian existence. It must flourish above all in the very heart of liturgy. But it cannot flourish where an activist spirit seeks to evade the deep inner demands and challenges of the Christian life in personal confrontation with God. This inner personal quest does not conflict with the mediating power of the Church, for the dread and guilt of the sinner show him more clearly than anything else his desperate need *for reconciliation with God in and through reconciliation with his brother*.

A dread that would merely thrust a man deeper into himself and into supposed contemplation is not yet serious. The only full and authentic purification is that which turns a man completely inside out, so that he no longer has a self to defend, no longer an intimate heritage to protect against imagined inroads and dilapidations. In other words (again following Gabriel Marcel), dread divests us of the sense of possession, of "having" our being and our power to love, in order that we may simply *be* in perfect openness (turned inside out), a defenselessness that is utter simplicity and total gift.

This is at once the heart of meditation and of liturgical sacrifice. It is the sign of the Spirit upon the Chosen People of God, not the ones who "have" an inner life and "deserve" respect in the gathering of an institution notorious for its piety, but who have simply surrendered to God in the desert of emptiness where he reveals his inutterable mercy without condition and without explanation in the mystery of Love.

Now we can understand that the full maturity of the spiritual life cannot be reached unless we first pass through the dread, anguish, trouble and fear that necessarily accompany the inner crisis of "spiritual death" in which we finally abandon our attachment to our exterior self and surrender completely to Christ. But when this surrender has been truly made, there is no longer any place for fear and dread. There can no longer be any doubt or hesitation in the mind of one who is completely and finally resolved to seek nothing and do nothing but what is willed for him by God's love. Then, as St. Benedict says,[72] "perfect love casts out dread," and dread itself is turned into love, confidence and hope.

The purpose of the dark night, as St. John of the Cross shows, is not simply to punish and afflict the heart of man, but to liberate, to purify and to enlighten in perfect love. The way that leads through dread goes not to despair but to perfect joy, not to hell but to heaven.

> Therefore, O spiritual soul, when you see your desire obscured, your affections arid and constrained, and your faculties bereft of their capacity for any interior exercise, be not afflicted by this, but rather consider it a great happiness, since God is freeing you from yourself and taking the work from your hands. For with those hands, howsoever well they may serve you, you would never labor so effectively, so perfectly and so securely (because of their clumsiness and uncleanness) as now, when God takes your hand and guides you in the darkness, as though you were blind, to an end and by a way which you know not nor could you ever hope to travel with the aid of your own eyes and feet, howsoever good you may be as a walker.[73]

72. Rule, end of Chapter 7.
73. *Dark Night*, II, xvi, 7.

XIX

IS THE Christian life of prayer simply an evasion of the problems and anxieties of contemporary existence? If what we have said has been properly understood, the answer to this question should be quite obvious. If we pray "in the Spirit" we are certainly not running away from life, negating visible reality in order to "see God." For "the Spirit of the Lord has filled the whole earth." Prayer does not blind us to the world, but it transforms our vision of the world, and makes us see it, all men, and all the history of mankind, in the light of God. To pray "in spirit and in truth" enables us to enter into contact with that infinite love, that inscrutable freedom which is at work behind the complexities and the intricacies of human existence. This does not mean fabricating for ourselves pious rationalizations to explain everything that happens. It involves no surreptitious manipulation of the hard truths of life.

139

Meditation does not necessarily give us a privileged insight into the meaning of isolated historical events. These can remain for the Christian as much of an agonizing mystery as they do for anyone else. But for us the mystery contains, within its own darkness and its own silences, a presence and a meaning which we apprehend without fully understanding them. And by this spiritual contact, this act of faith, we are ourselves properly situated in the events around us, even though we may not quite see where they are going.

One thing is certain: the humility of faith, if it is followed by the proper consequences—by the acceptance of the work and sacrifice demanded by our providential task—will do far more to launch us into the full current of historical reality than the pompous rationalizations of politicians who think they are somehow the directors and manipulators of history. Politicians may indeed make history, but the meaning of what they are making turns out, inexorably, to have been something in a language they will never understand, which contradicts their own programs and turns all their achievements into an absurd parody of their promises and ideals.

Of course, it is true that religion on a superficial level, religion that is untrue to itself and to God, easily comes to serve as the "opium of the people." And this takes place whenever religion and prayer invoke the name of God for reasons and ends that have nothing to do with him. When religion becomes a mere artificial facade to justify a social or economic system—when religion hands over its rites and language completely to the political propagandist, and when prayer becomes the vehicle for a purely secular ideological program, then religion does tend to become an opiate. It deadens the spirit enough to permit the substitution of a superficial fiction and mythology for this truth of life. And this brings about the alienation of the believer, so that his religious zeal becomes political fanaticism. His faith in God, while preserving its traditional formulas, becomes in fact faith in his own nation, class or race. His ethic ceases to be the law of God and of love, and becomes the law that might-makes-right: established privilege justifies everything. God is the *status quo*.

In the last book to come to us from the hand of Raïssa Maritain, her commentary on the Lord's Prayer, we read the following passage, concerning those who barely obtain their daily bread, and are deprived of most of the advantages of a decent life on earth by the injustice and thoughtlessness of the privileged:

If there were fewer wars, less thirst to dominate and to exploit others, less national egoism, less egoism of class and caste, if man were more concerned for his brother, and really wanted to collect together, for the good of the human race, all the resources which science places at his disposal especially today, there would be on earth fewer populations deprived of their necessary sustenance, there would be fewer children who die or are incurably weakened by undernourishment.[74]

She goes on to ask what obstacles man has placed in the way of the Gospel that this should be so. It is unfortunately true that those who have complacently

74. *Notes sur le Pater* (Paris, 1962), p. 98.

imagined themselves blessed by God have in fact done more than others to frustrate his will. But Raïssa Maritain says that perhaps the poor, who have never been able to seek the kingdom of God, may be found by it "when they leave the world which has not recognized in them the image of God."[75]

Religion always tends to lose its inner consistency and its supernatural truth when it lacks the fervor of contemplation. It is the contemplative, silent, "empty" and apparently useless element in the life of prayer which makes it truly a *life*. Without contemplation, liturgy tends to be a mere pious show and para-liturgical prayer is plain babbling. Without contemplation, mental prayer is nothing but a sterile exercise of the mind. And yet not everyone can be a "contemplative." That is not the point. What matters is the *contemplative orientation* of the whole life of prayer.

If the contemplative orientation of prayer is its emptiness, its "uselessness," its purity, then we can say that prayer tends to lose its true character in so far as it becomes busy, full of ulterior purposes, and committed to programs that are beneath its own level. Now this does not mean that we can never "pray for" particular goods. We can and must use the prayer of petition, and this is even compatible, in a very simple and pure form, with the spirit of contemplation.

One can pass from the prayer of petition directly into contemplation when one has a very profound faith and a great simplicity of theological hope.[76] *But when prayer allows itself to be exploited* for purposes which are

75. *Ibid.,* p. 100.
76. St. John of the Cross identifies this hope with the night, or emptiness, of the memory.

142

beneath itself and have nothing directly to do with our life in God, or our life on earth oriented to God, then it becomes strictly impure.

Prayer must penetrate and enliven every department of our life, including that which is most temporal and transient. Prayer does not despise even the seemingly lowliest aspects of man's temporal existence. It spiritualizes all of them and gives them a divine orientation. But prayer is defiled when it is turned away from God and from the spirit, and manipulated in the interests of group fanaticism.

In such cases, religion is understood to be at least implicitly misdirected, and therefore the "God" whom it invokes becomes, or tends to become, a mere figment of the imagination. Such religion is insincere. It is merely a front for greed, injustice, sensuality, selfishness, violence. The cure for this corruption is to restore the purity of faith and the genuineness of Christian love: and this means a restoration of the contemplative orientation of prayer.

Real contemplatives will always be rare and few. But that is not a matter of importance, as long as the whole Church is predominantly contemplative in all her teaching, all her activity and all her prayer. There is no contradiction between action and contemplation when Christian apostolic activity is raised to the level of pure charity. On that level, action and contemplation are fused into one entity by the love of God and of our brother in Christ. But the trouble is that if prayer is not itself deep, powerful and pure and filled at all times with the spirit of contemplation, Christian action can never really reach this high level.

Without the spirit of contemplation in all our worship

—that is to say without the adoration and love of God above all, for his own sake, because he is God—the liturgy will not nourish a really Christian apostolate based on Christ's love and carried out in the power of the *Pneuma*.

The most important need in the Christian world today is this inner truth nourished by this Spirit of contemplation: the praise and love of God, the longing for the coming of Christ, the thirst for the manifestation of God's glory, his truth, his justice, his Kingdom in the world. These are all characteristically "contemplative" and eschatological aspirations of the Christian heart, and they are the very essence of monastic prayer. Without them our apostolate is more for our own glory than for the glory of God.

Without this contemplative orientation we are building churches not to praise him but to establish more firmly the social structures, values and benefits that we presently enjoy. Without this contemplative basis to our preaching, our apostolate is no apostolate at all, but mere proselytizing to insure universal conformity with our own national way of life.

Without contemplation and interior prayer the Church cannot fulfill her mission to transform and save mankind. Without contemplation, she will be reduced to being the servant of cynical and worldly powers, no matter how hard her faithful may protest that they are fighting for the Kingdom of God.

Without true, deep contemplative aspirations, without a total love for God and an uncompromising thirst for his truth, religion tends in the end to become an opiate.